Building English Skills

Purple Level

Yellow Level

Blue Level

Orange Level

Green Level

Red Level

Gold Level

Silver Level

Aqua Level

BROWN LEVEL

Plum Level

Pink Level

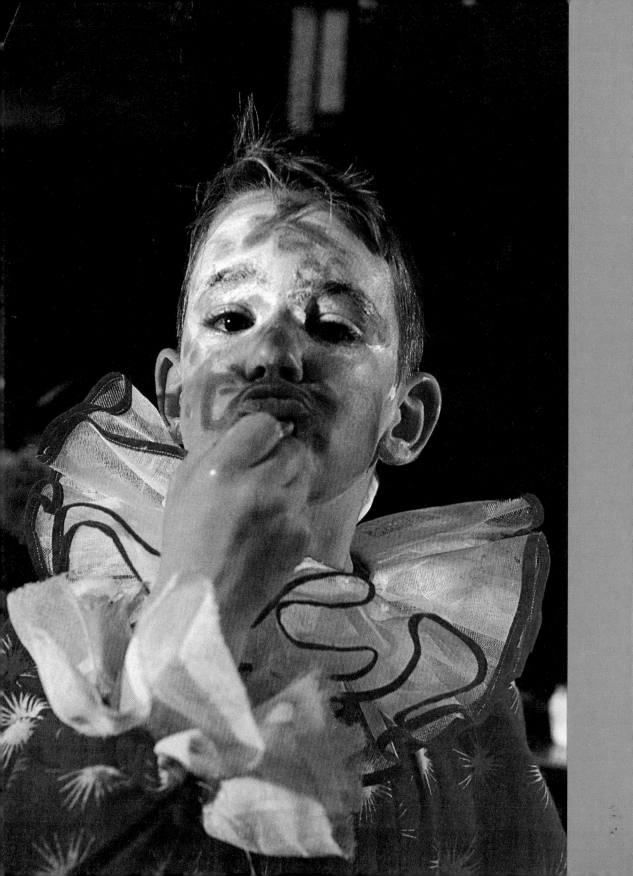

Building English Skills

Brown Level

McDougal, Littell & Company

Evanston, Illinois

Sacramento, California

Authors

Frances Freeman Paden, Consultant in Language and Speech,
Evanston, Illinois

Susan Duffy Schaffrath, Consultant in Educational Materials for the Elementary
and Middle Grades, Chicago, Illinois

Sandra D. Wittenbrink, Teacher and Writer, Evanston, Illinois

Consultants

Phyllis W. Dole, Language Arts Consultant and Teacher, San Juan
Capistrano, California

Murial N. Stanek, Consultant in Language Arts, Wilmette, Illinois

Sally Todd, Teacher, District 109, Deerfield, Illinois

Editorial Direction: Joy Littell

Associate Editor: Patricia Opaskar

Design: William A. Seabright

Acknowledgments: See page 310.

ISBN: 0–88343–500–4

Contents

Handbook

Chapter 1

Our Growing Language

The words we use make up our language. The English language has more than half a million words. We are always making new words. New words make our language grow and change.

These new words come from many places. Some words come from sounds. Some words come from other languages. Some words are made from other words.

In this chapter, you will find out where words come from. You will learn about many kinds of words.

1

Part 1 Words That Come from Sounds

Many words in our language come from sounds. You hear the real sound in these words. They *echo* the sounds. These words are called **echoic words.** Here are some examples of echoic words. Say each word aloud. Listen to the sound it makes.

pop   hum   thump
crash   swish   buzz
boom   growl   purr

Listen to the sound of the word *pop.* It echoes a real sound. When you make popcorn, you hear the *pop* sound. When you break a balloon, you hear a *pop.*
The word *growl* also echoes a real sound. A lion may growl. An angry dog often growls.

Exercises Using Words That Come from Sounds

A. Here is a list of echoic words. Each word echoes a real sound. The second list tells what makes the sounds. Number your paper from 1 to 8 and write the words. Then write the matching sound for each word.

> Sample echoic word buzz
> > Possible sound the sound of a bee

1. boom   a. the sound of rain
2. crackle   b. the sound of thunder
3. rip   c. the sound of a blazing fire
4. drip   d. the sound of a loud bell
5. fizz   e. the sound of cloth tearing
6. purr   f. the sound of a happy cat
7. clang   g. the sound of a car horn
8. honk   h. the sound of a bubbly soda

B. Here is a list of five echoic words. Beside it is a list of five sounds. Number your paper from 1 to 5 and write the echoic words. After each word, write the sound it matches.

> Sample echoic word clip-clop
> > Matching sound a horse walking on a street

1. thump   a. water pouring from a bottle
2. splash   b. a piece of metal hitting another
3. gurgle   c. a fingernail scratching a
                  chalkboard
4. screech   d. a heavy rock falling into a lake
5. clank   e. a ball bouncing

3

Part 2 Words Borrowed from Other Languages

The English language **borrows** many new words from other languages. Some of these languages are American Indian, Spanish, French, Italian, Dutch, and German.

When the first settlers came to America, they learned many new words from the American Indians. The Indians taught them their names for trees, fruits, and vegetables. For example, the Indians taught the settlers the word *squash*. The Indians also learned new words from the settlers.

Since that time, people from all over the world have come to our country. Each group of people brought a whole new set of words. The French people brought such words as *grand*, *ballet*, and *fabric*. The German people brought the word *kindergarten*. The Dutch people brought the word *dock*. After a while, these words became part of the English language.

We also borrow new words from our neighbors. Mexico is our neighbor to the South. In Mexico most people speak Spanish. We have borrowed many Spanish words from our neighbors in Mexico. The Mexicans have borrowed many English words from us. It is a kind of trade. All countries borrow and trade words to add to their languages.

Here is a chart. It gives some examples of words borrowed from other languages.

American Indian	Spanish/ Mexican	French
canoe	ranch	pumpkin
skunk	rodeo	lake
moose	patio	magic
coyote	gusto	button

Dutch	German	African
freight	dachshund	banjo
easel	pretzel	okra
landscape	delicatessen	gnu
stoop	loafer	marimba

Exercise **Using Words Borrowed from Other Languages**

Here are nine food words that came from other countries. Can you guess where each word came from?

won ton   spaghetti   frankfurter

taco   chili   tamale

strudel   pizza   gumbo

Part 3 Words Made from Other Words

In the English language, new words are being made all the time. Many of the new words have been "built." They are words made from other words. There are several ways to build new words.

Some words are made up of two different words. Two words are put together to make the new word. The new word must make sense. The new word is called a **compound word**. The English language has many compound words. New compound words are being made all the time.

pea + nut = peanut   foot + ball = football

dish + water = dishwater   pen + pal = pen pal

home + work = homework   base + ball = baseball

Exercise Using Compound Words

Here is a list of six words. Each is a *compound word*. Each word is made up of two different words. Number your paper from 1 to 6. Write the two words that make up each compound word.

Sample compound word sailboat

Answer sail + boat

6

1. highway   4. toenail
2. bedtime   5. doorknob
3. toothbrush   6. playground

Part 4 Building New Words

There are more ways to make new words from other words. New parts can be added to a word to make a new word.

Prefixes

One way to build a new word is to add a part to the beginning of a word. Here is an example.

Part	Word	New Word
re	+ make	= remake

The part *re* added to the word *make* makes a new word, *remake*. The part that is added is called a *prefix*. A **prefix** is added to the *beginning* of a word. It changes the meaning of the word. It builds a new word.

The prefix *re* means "again." What does *remake* mean?

Here is another example of how the prefix *re* builds a new word.

> Mary must *do* her work.
> Mary must *redo* her work.

In the second sentence, Mary has done her work. Now she must redo it, or "do it again." The prefix *re* has built a new word. It has changed the meaning of the word *do*. It has changed the meaning of the sentence.

7

Here is another prefix. The prefix *un* means "not."
Read this example of how the prefix *un* builds a
new word.

Jim is *happy.*
Jim is *unhappy.*

In the second sentence, Jim is unhappy, or "not
happy." The prefix *un* has built a new word. It has
changed the meaning of the word *happy.* It has
changed the meaning of the sentence.

Exercise   Using Prefixes

Here are six descriptions. Number your paper from 1 to 6.
Write a new word that means the same thing as each
description. Use a prefix in your new word.

Sample description not clear
New word unclear

1. not tied   4. write again
2. wrap again   5. use again
4. not painted   6. not finished

Suffixes

Another way to build a new word is to add a part at the end of a word. Here is an example.

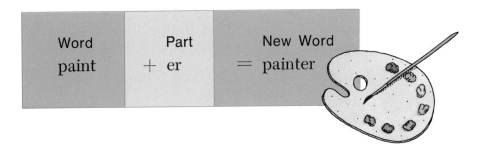

Word	Part	New Word
paint	+ er	= painter

The part *er* added to the end of the word *paint* makes a new word, *painter*. The part that is added is called a *suffix*. A **suffix** is added to the *end* of a word. It changes the meaning of the word. It builds a new word.

The suffix *er* means "a person or thing who does something." What does *painter* mean?

Here is another example of how the suffix *er* builds a new word.

My mother likes to *garden*.
My mother is a *gardener*.

In the first sentence, the word *garden* means "to take care of a place with fruits, flowers, or vegetables." In the second sentence, the word *gardener* means "a person who takes care of a place with fruits, flowers, or vegetables." The suffix *er* has changed the meaning of the word *garden*.

9

Here is another suffix. The suffix *less* means "without." Read this example of how it is used.

I have a new *tooth*.
The old dog was *toothless*.

The first sentence uses *tooth* in a way you understand. The second sentence says that the old dog was "without" a tooth. He had no teeth. The suffix *less* has changed the meaning of the word *tooth*.

Exercises   Building New Words

A. Here are six descriptions. Number your paper from 1 to 6. Write a new word that means the same thing as each description. Use a suffix in your new word.

Sample description without end
New word endless

1. without time
2. without help
3. someone who calls
4. someone who works
5. someone who reads
6. without use

B. Here are six descriptions. Number your paper from 1 to 6. Write a new word that means the same thing as each description. Use a prefix or a suffix in your new word.

Sample description someone who drives
New word driver

1. someone who teaches
2. without care
3. someone who speaks
4. not wrapped
5. run again
6. heat again

hippopotamus   rhinoceros

Part 5   Short Words from Long Words

We get some new words by shortening long words. We use only a part of the word. For example, we say *burger* for *hamburger,* and *movies* for *moving pictures.* The part of the word becomes a new word all by itself. Using only a part of a long word is called **clipping.** We clip, or cut off, a piece of the word.

Exercise   Making Short Words from Long Words

Here are the long forms of nine English words. Number your paper from 1 to 9. Next to each number, write the clipped form of each word.

Sample word zoological garden
Clipped word zoo

1. photograph
2. telephone
3. frankfurter
4. mathematics
5. gymnasium
6. taxicab
7. milkshake
8. automobile
9. airplane

11

Our Growing Language

A. Using Words That Came from Sounds
(Use after page 3.)

Here is a list of five echoic words. Beside it is a list of five sounds. Number your paper from 1 to 5 and write the echoic words. After each word, write the sound it matches.

1. bang   a. a baby bird
2. sniff   b. walking through mud
3. squish   c. a railroad engine
4. peep   d. a firecracker
5. chug   e. breathing while crying

B. Using Words Borrowed from Other Languages
(Use after page 5.)

Here are five stories of words borrowed from other languages. Number your paper from 1 to 5. Next to each number write the English word.

1. When the Spanish came to South America, they found a new food. The people in South America called it *batata*. The Spanish called it *patata*. English borrowed the word from Spanish. What is it?

2. Long ago, the Chinese used a sauce called *ke-tsiap* on fish. We have a tomato sauce that is used on hamburgers. It is not the same as the Chinese sauce, but we borrowed the Chinese word for it. What is it?

3. The French word for an axe is *hache*. English borrowed this word to use as a name for a small axe. What do we call a small axe?

4. The Arabic word for a journey is *safar*. Swahili borrowed this word, and English borrowed it from Swahili. In English it also means a journey. What is it?

5. What North American animal wears a mask? It uses its front paws like hands. Algonquin Indians called it *arakun*, which means "scratches with hands." English borrowed the word. What is the animal?

C. Building New Words   (Use after page 10.)

Number your paper from 1 to 9. Next to each number, write *suffix* if the word has a suffix added to it. Write *prefix* if the word has a prefix added. Tell what each word means.

Sample word **reader**

Explanation suffix—**reader** means "someone who reads"

1. unhurt	4. helpless	7. leader
2. rewrite	5. farmer	8. unkind
3. unable	6. remake	9. singer

D. Making Short Words from Long Words
(Use after page 11.)

Here are the long forms of six English words. Number your paper from 1 to 6. Next to each number, write the clipped form of each word.

13

1. airplane	3. omnibus	5. examination
2. luncheon	4. gasoline	6. gymnasium

Chapter 2

Learning New Words

What do you do if you meet a new word in your reading? That happens to everybody at some time. It is important to find out what the new word means. Learning new words will help you understand more of what you read.

Sometimes you can figure out a new word by taking it apart. As you have learned, some words are compound words. Others use prefixes and suffixes to change the meaning of words you already know.

However, there are other words you cannot figure out in that way. This chapter will show you other ways to find their meanings.

Part 1 Using a Dictionary

A good way to get help with a new word is to use a dictionary. A dictionary can tell you the meanings of words. It can show you how words are used in sentences. It can teach you many other things. First, you must learn how to use the dictionary. This chapter will show you how.

Alphabetical Order

Words in a dictionary are in alphabetical order. Alphabetical order depends on the first letters of words. The words are listed in the way the letters are listed in the alphabet. This helps you find words easily. Words beginning with *A* are first. *B* words come next. Then come *C* words, and so on. Here are some groups of letters in alphabetical order.

Group 1	Group 2	Group 3
a	a	c
b	b	r
c	s	s

Here are some groups of words in alphabetical order.

Group 1	Group 2	Group 3
apple	airplane	crawl
banana	bus	run
cherry	ship	swim

The dictionary is not the only book that uses alphabetical order. Telephone books also use it. Many other lists and books use alphabetical order. Knowing how alphabetical order works is very helpful.

Exercise   Using Alphabetical Order

Here are six lists of words. Put each list of words into alphabetical order.

1. animal	2. snack	3. sun
fish	breakfast	rain
bird	lunch	clouds
person	dinner	wind
insect	meal	breeze

4. desk	5. orange	6. eraser
chair	purple	crayon
table	green	pencil
shelf	blue	book
chalk	yellow	ruler

Finding a Word in a Dictionary

Suppose you hear a new word. You want to look it up in the dictionary. How can you find it? You need to learn to open the dictionary at the right place.

Open your dictionary about in the middle. About half of the alphabet is on the left side. About half is on the right side. When you open your dictionary in the middle, you should see *L* words or *M* words. These letters are in the middle of the alphabet.

The following picture shows where you would look to find pages with a certain beginning letter. Letters near the beginning of the alphabet are near the front of the book. Letters near the end of the alphabet are near the end of the book.

Exercises Opening a Dictionary at the Right Place

A. Choose a partner. Practice opening the dictionary to a certain letter. Ask your partner to say a letter. Then, you try to open the dictionary to that letter. Take turns with your partner. Practice until both of you can open the book close to the right letter.

B. Fold a piece of paper in half the long way. Write *First Half of Alphabet* on one half of your paper. Write *Second Half of Alphabet* on the other half. Look at the picture above to see where you would find each letter. Copy each of these words. Put each one on the correct side.

feather	happy	window	root
beak	sad	door	stem
wing	afraid	floor	leaf
tail	unhappy	roof	plant

Using Guide Words

At the top of every dictionary page are two **guide words** in large letters. The guide word at the left tells the first word listed on that page. The guide word at the right tells the last word listed on that page.

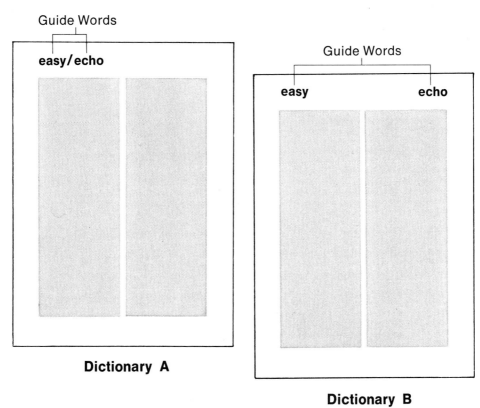

Guide Words

easy/echo

Dictionary A

Guide Words

easy   **echo**

Dictionary B

First Word on Page   **easy**

Last Word on Page   **echo**

When you are looking for a certain word, the guide words can help you. You must find the guide words closest in alphabetical order to your word. Then look through the words on that page for your word.

For example, suppose you are looking for the word *song*. You would first find the S pages of your dictionary. Then you would look for guide words that begin with *so*.

Here are the guide words for two pages of a dictionary. Which page has the word *song*?

1	2
solo—some	somebody—soon

Both sets of guide words begin with *so*. Therefore, you must look at the third letter of each guide word. Remember that the word you are looking for, *song* begins with *son*.

The guide words in the first set begin with *sol* and *som*. Does *son* come between *sol* and *som*? No, *n* comes after both *l* and *m*. Therefore *song* comes on a page after the page with these guide words.

The guide words in the second set begin with *som* and *soo*. Does *son* come between *som* and *soo*? Yes, *n* is after *m*, and before *o*. Therefore, *song* comes on the page with the guide words *somebody* and *soon*.

Sometimes you turn too many pages and go past the page you want. Suppose you came to a page with the guide words *soot* and *sound*. Would *song* be on a page before or after that page? Look at the third letter of each word. Think of alphabetical order. *N* comes before both *o* and *u*. Therefore *song* comes on a page before the page with the guide words *soot* and *sound*.

Where will you find **gold**?

get	give

go	gum

Exercises Using Guide Words

A. Number your paper from 1 to 6. Six of the following words are on one page of a dictionary. The page has the guide words *mold* and *money*. Find the six words that belong on that page. Copy those words.

move	nest	molt
mole	man	me
open	money	moment
mom	monkey	moldy

B. After each of the following words, there are two sets of guide words. Number your paper from 1 to 10. Read each word. Choose the pair of guide words that will be on the page with that word. Copy the guide words you have chosen.

1. beetle	beckon—before	bass—batter
2. circle	chubby—circle	civil—clap
3. grace	greeting—grind	grab—graft
4. expert	end—engineer	expel—explore
5. hickory	hiss—hive	hexagon—high
6. paddle	padding—pair	pace—pad
7. decoy	declare—deduct	drip—drop
8. football	fond—for	forge—form
9. marlin	marathon—mark	mark—marry
10. tenor	temple—tender	tendon—term

Finding the Meaning of a Word

The dictionary tells the meaning of each word it lists. The words are printed in heavy black letters. The meaning is printed in lighter letters after the word.

Here is a sample page from a dictionary. How many words are listed? Can you find their meanings?

hasp a metal piece that swings on a hinge and fits over a staple through which a pin or lock is passed to keep a door, window, or lid closed.

has sock a firm cushion used as a footstool or low seat.

haste 1. the act of hurrying; quick movement or action [She left in *haste*.] 2. a hurrying in a careless way [*Haste* makes waste.]

hast y done or made with haste; hurried.

hat a covering for the head, usually with a brim and a crown.

hatch 1. to bring forth young birds, fish, turtles, etc. from eggs [Birds *hatch* their eggs by keeping them warm.] 2. to come forth from the egg [Our chicks *hatched* this morning.] 3. to think up or plan, often in a secret or bad way [They *hatched* a plot to rob the bank.]

hatch back an automobile body with a rear panel that swings up.

hatch er y a place for hatching eggs, as of fish or hens.

hatch et a small ax with a short handle.

hate 1. to have very bad feeling against; dislike very much [to *hate* an enemy; to *hate* to clean house] 2. a very strong dislike.

ha tred a very strong dislike; hate.

hat ter a person who makes or sells men's hats.

haul 1. to move by pulling; drag or tug [We *hauled* the boat up on the beach.] 2. to carry by wagon, truck, etc. [He *hauls* steel for a large company.]

Ha van a the capital of Cuba.

have 1. to be the owner of; possess [They *have* red hair.] 2. to contain

Notice that the dictionary uses different ways to explain meanings.

1. The dictionary may simply tell the meaning of a word. Look at **hassock** on the sample page. Can you find another word with only a meaning after it?

2. The dictionary may give example sentences to make the meaning clearer. Look at **haste** on the sample page. Can you find any other words with example sentences?

3. The dictionary may give a picture of a word. Look at **hasp** on the sample page. What other word is pictured?

Sometimes a word may have several meanings. The dictionary usually gives numbers to the different meanings of a word. For example, read the meanings of **hatch.** When there is more than one meaning, you should read all of the meanings. Think of how the word is used in the sentence in which you found it. Choose the meaning that fits the sentence best.

Exercises   Finding the Meaning of a Word

A. Number your paper from 1 to 10. Each of the following sentences has one word missing. Choose the word from the sample dictionary page that fits in each sentence. Write the missing word.

1. Dad rested his feet on a _____.
2. Robins _____ their eggs in the spring.
3. Our new car is a _____.

4. We are late, so do a _____ job washing the dishes.

5. I spilled my paint because of my _____.

6. The wind blew Mom's _____ from her head.

7. The woodman used a _____ to cut down the tree.

8. That truck will _____ frozen food to grocery stores.

9. I _____ to be late for a movie.

10. The door swung open because the _____ was broken.

B. Number your paper from 1 to 3. Each of the following sentences uses a different meaning of *hatch.* For each sentence, choose the best meaning of *hatch* from the sample dictionary page. Write the number of the best meaning after the number of the sentence.

1. The robbers met to <u>hatch</u> a plan of action.

2. Turtles <u>hatch</u> their eggs by burying them in warm sand.

3. The father penguin holds the egg on his feet until it <u>hatches</u>.

Part 2　Finding Clues to Meanings

You do not always need a dictionary to understand a new word. Sometimes the sentence where you found the word can help you. It gives you clues. The clues can help you decide what the word means. Be sure to study the sentence. Here are some ways the writer helps you.

1. Sometimes the writer tells you the meaning of a new word in the rest of the sentence. Here is an example.

> The ax made a <u>gash</u>, or long deep cut, in the tree.

The writer thinks you might need help with the word *gash*. What does the sentence tell you? It tells you that a *gash* is a long, deep cut.

Other times the writer tells you the meaning of a new word in a separate sentence. Here is an example.

> Have you ever seen the <u>Milky Way</u>? It is a group of millions of stars.

The writer explains what the Milky Way is. The second sentence tells you that the Milky Way is a group of millions of stars.

2. Sometimes you can use the information given in other sentences to find the meaning of a word. Here is an example.

> <u>Hail</u> fell during the storm. Hail is small, round pieces of ice.

The writer helps you understand what *hail* is. The first sentence tells you that hail falls during a storm. The second sentence tells you that hail is small, round pieces of ice. The two sentences tell you that hail is a special kind of ice that falls during storms.

3. Sometimes a writer only gives you clues to the meaning of a new word. You must think about the information given in the sentences around a new word. Then you can decide what the new word probably means.

Here is an example.

The zoo keeper held a <u>cony</u> in his hand. A cony is furry and looks like a guinea pig.

Do you know the meaning of *cony?* The writer gives you some clues. What does a zoo keeper do? What kind of animal would be furry? Do the sentences give a clue about the animal's size? Now can you make a good guess about a cony? Here is another example.

My little brother is a <u>mimic</u>. He often copies other people's actions.

The writer helps you find out what a *mimic* is. The first sentence tells you that the brother is a mimic. The second sentence tells more about the little brother. You can put together the two ideas. Then you can figure out what *mimic* means. Did you decide that a mimic is a person who copies other people's actions?

Exercise Finding Clues to Meanings

Number your paper from 1 to 10. Here are some sets of sentences. Each set has a word that may be new to you. These words are underlined. Some sets of sentences give the meaning of the new word. Others give clues about the meaning. Study the sentences. Decide what you think each new word means. Write the new words and their meanings on your paper.

1. In the garden are some ladybirds, small red bugs with spotted backs.

2. At the pet store I saw a newt, a lizard that can live on land or in water.

3. My shoes are made of kid. Kid is the skin of goats.

4. Did you ever see a llama, an animal like a camel without a hump?

5. Please don't heckle. Don't ask questions and tease when someone is talking.

6. The earth tremor lasted ten seconds. It shook apart many buildings.

7. Dripping water irks me. Another noise that bothers me is a fingernail scraping the chalkboard.

8. The sun is at its zenith at noon. Its zenith is its highest point.

9. This horse can vault high fences. It can jump over fences six feet high.

10. Carl paints portraits. Debbie, Walter, and Helen are some of the people whose pictures he has painted.

More Exercises

Learning New Words

A. Using a Dictionary   (Use after page 23.)

Look at this part of a dictionary page. Find the parts asked for below. Number your paper from 1 to 6. Write parts asked for.

---

key   **kidnap**

key 1. a small metal device that one puts into a lock and turns so as to lock or unlock a door, drawer, etc. 2. a certain manner, tone, or style [Her letter was in a cheerful *key*.] 3. any one of the flat parts, buttons, etc, that are pressed.

kg or **kg.** the short way of writing kilogram or kilograms.
khaki 1. yellowish brown. 2. a strong, heavy cotton cloth of this color.

---

1. What are the guide words on this page?

2. Write one word listed on this dictionary page.

3. What is the meaning of *kg?*

4. What example sentence is given on the dictionary page above?

5. Look at the meanings for *key*. Write the number of the meaning that best fits this sentence.

The janitor used his *key* to let us in.

6. Look at the meanings for *khaki*. Write the number of the meaning that best fits this sentence.

Her uniform was made of *khaki*.

28

B. Finding Clues to Meanings   (Use after page 26.)

Number your paper from 1 to 10. Here are some sets of sentences. Each set has a word that may be new to you. These words are underlined. Some sets of sentences give the meaning of the new word. Others give clues about the meaning. Study the sentences. Decide what you think each word means. Write the new words and their meanings on your paper.

1. The old man told us a yarn, a story that is hard to believe.

2. Eagles have sharp talons, or claws.

3. My grandmother makes pickles in a crock. A crock is a pot or jar.

4. The horse nibbled at tufts of grass. A tuft is a bunch of something.

5. He cinched his new belt around his waist. He buckled it tightly.

6. Fozzie and Kermit came to a fork in the road. Here the road split into two different roads.

7. The balloon ascended slowly. As it floated upward, the crowd cheered.

8. My aunt is a resident of Richmond Apartments. She has lived there for two years.

9. We laughed at the clown's antics, or tricks.

10. This puzzle is an octagon. Its eight sides makes it hard to put together.

Chapter 3

Talking with Others

Your friends are important to you. You like to be with them. You talk things over with them. You listen to their ideas. In this chapter you will learn more about sharing ideas and feelings with other people.

Sometimes you want your friends to meet each other. You want them to be able to talk together, too. To help them get to know one another, you need to make introductions.

Part 1 Making Introductions

You are helpful when you introduce people. You help them know each other. Let's see how José introduces two people he especially likes.

> José's mother has come to Parent's Day at school. José wants to introduce his mother to his teacher. Here is what he says.
>
> "Mom, I'd like you to meet my teacher, Ms. Davis. She has been helping me learn to write better."
>
> Then José turns to his teacher. He says, "Ms. Davis, this is my mother. Her name is Ms. Fernandez."

Now let's think about José's introduction.

First, José presented his mother to his teacher. He introduced his teacher by saying her name. He also told his mother something about his teacher. What did he say?

Next, José introduced his mother. He said his mother's name was Ms. Fernandez.

Do you know why you should introduce your parents by name? Why didn't José just say, "This is my mother"?

Here is another introduction. Carol wants to help her friend meet new people. Here is what she does.

Carol has a new neighbor. Her name is Laura. Carol takes Laura with her on the first day of school. She wants Laura to meet some of her friends. When Carol sees Amy and Jack, she calls them over.

"Amy! Jack! I want you to meet my new neighbor, Laura. She just moved here from Florida."

Then Carol turns to Laura. She says, "Laura, these are my friends. Jack lives on our street. Amy comes to my house sometimes. Amy and I take dancing lessons together."

Carol knew that Laura might feel shy. She helped her. Carol told Amy and Jack something about Laura. What did she say?

What did Carol tell Laura about Amy and Jack?

You should always say more than names when you introduce people. You should think of something interesting to say about each person. In this way, you will make it easier for people to start talking.

Here are some guides to remember when you introduce people.

Guides for Making Introductions

1. Look at the people you are introducing.

2. Say the names of the people you want to introduce.

3. Tell something about each person you introduce.

Exercise   Making Introductions

Work in groups of three. Act out one of these introductions. Follow the Guides for Making Introductions.

1. Susan's father, Mr. Gordon, comes to Lincoln School. Susan introduces her father to her teacher. Susan's teacher is Mr. Franco.

2. Tommy arrives for his first day of school. The only person he knows is Diana. Diana greets Tommy. Then she introduces him to her friend Meg.

3. The class has been studying careers. Karen has invited her cousin, a TV newscaster, to visit the room. There she introduces her cousin to her friend Dave.

Part 2 Carrying On a Conversation

Once people know something about each other, they usually begin to talk. If they are friendly, they have many things to share.

However, to keep a conversation going is not always easy. You must keep your mind on what people are saying. It is important to listen to others and ask questions.

Read this conversation between three good friends.

POLLY: I got some new roller skates for my birthday.

TIM: That's great. Have you ever skated before?

POLLY: I learned last summer. Ever since then, I've wanted skates.

LIZ: Maybe we could all go skating on Saturday.

TIM: You could come to my house. We have a long driveway.

POLLY: Thanks, Tim. I'll ask my parents.

LIZ: So will I. I don't have any skates, but I think I can borrow my sister's.

TIM: I'll check with my parents, too. I think it will be okay.

POLLY: Let's get together tomorrow to make final plans.

Now think about the conversation. Several good things happened in it.

Polly began by telling about her new skates. Then Tim asked a question. How did Tim's question help keep the conversation going?

In this conversation everyone took turns talking. Sometimes that is hard to do. You must be careful not to interrupt when you are talking in a group.

These guides will help you have good conversations with your friends.

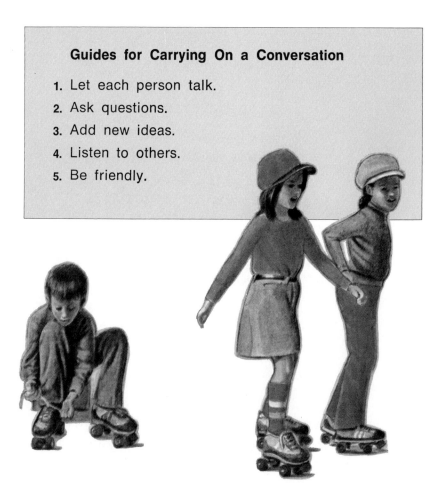

Guides for Carrying On a Conversation

1. Let each person talk.
2. Ask questions.
3. Add new ideas.
4. Listen to others.
5. Be friendly.

Exercises   Carrying On a Conversation

A. Read this conversation. Then divide into groups of three. Choose parts. Act out the conversation.

PAM: My goldfish aren't doing very well.

BLAKE: Maybe you need to clean their bowl.

JERRY: You never take care of your animals, Pam.

PAM: Yes, I do. Does anyone know if fish need vitamins?

BLAKE: Sometimes they need a special food. Mr. Johnson can tell you about that.

PAM: I'll go to see him after school.

JERRY: I'm tired of hearing about your fish.

B. Answer these questions about "Taking Care of Fish." Write your answers on your paper. Then talk about your answers with the other people in your group.

1. Jerry says, "You never take care of your animals, Pam." How does Jerry make Pam feel?

2. Pam answers Jerry. Then she goes on with the conversation. What question does she ask?

3. Jerry says, "I'm tired of hearing about your fish." Was Jerry friendly?

4. After Jerry's remark, the conversation needs a new idea. Pretend you are joining the group. What would you say?

Part 3 Talking on the Telephone

Sometimes your conversations take place on the telephone. Of course, on the phone you and your friends can't see each other. You must speak and listen very carefully to keep the message clear.

Here's what happens when the phone rings in Tony's house.

TONY:	Hello.
VOICE:	Hello. This is Jeff. May I speak with Tony, please?
TONY:	Hi, Jeff. This is Tony.
VOICE:	Hi, Tony. Can you go to the park with me?
TONY:	Just a minute, please. I'll ask Mom. (Tony puts the receiver down gently. He asks his mother for permission to go to the park. Then he returns to the phone.)
TONY:	Jeff? Mom says OK. I'll meet you there in ten minutes.
VOICE:	Great! See you then, Tony.
TONY:	'Bye, Jeff.
VOICE:	Goodbye.

Tony and Jeff were polite to each other. What did Tony say when he had to leave the phone?

Remember to use your best manners on the telephone. If you have to leave the phone, say "Just a minute, please." Put the receiver down gently. Then return to the phone as quickly as you can.

Here are some guides. They will help you talk with others on the telephone.

Guides for Talking on the Telephone

1. When you pick up the phone, say hello.
2. If you are the caller, give your name. Tell why you are calling.
3. Listen carefully.
4. Speak clearly.
5. Say goodbye before you hang up.

Exercise   Talking on the Telephone

Divide into groups of four. Take turns acting out one of these phone calls. Be sure to follow the guides. When it is not your turn to act, listen to the others.

1. Emily calls Juan. She has a new bike. She wants to ride to Juan's house to show him her bike.

2. Maria calls Sarah. Maria's mother is going to teach her how to make raisin cookies. Maria wants Sarah to come over and learn, too.

3. Carlo calls Greg. Carlo needs some help raking leaves. He asks Greg to come over.

39

After you have acted out your phone call, ask your group to tell you how you did.

Part 4 Using the Phone Book

Sometimes you need to find a friend's phone number. You look it up in the phone book. In the phone book are names, addresses, and telephone numbers. The names are listed in alphabetical order, last name first. Children's names are not usually in the phone book.

Here is a sample page from a phone book.

Reese			Rental
Reese J 1605 Lee Av	269–6393	Rempas Jas 1205 College	428–7660
Reese John C		Remsberg Chas A	
530 Monticello Av	269–2963	1521 Rumson	364–5096
Reese Morris 2339 Taylor Av	675–0782	Rendleman Richard J Jr	
Reeser J Leonard		2001 Mayfield	269–5163
3259 Overlook	269–6857	Rene Jos 1041 Perry	892–9522
Reesh Chas E 2210 Randolph	428–9238	Renn David E 1149 McCoy	428–4709
Reeve C 118 Chelsea	364–8298	Renn R E 1929 Mayfield	175–6342
Reeve C 1812 Donald Av	364–4674	Renner Karl H 616 Belvoir	428–6096
Reeves H L 1927 Mayfield Av	175–8575	Rennord M 849 Lee Av	269–6989
Reeves Julian C Jr		Rensink Jas 1507 Green	269–3795
2746 Boynton Av	364–5651	Rent-Rite Equipment Company	
Reeves T Malcolm		1820 Lee Av	269–8011
2002 Euclid Av	269–8175	Rental Specialties	
Regan C A 1713 W. 4th	291–1638	1713 Donald	269–2260

Guide words appear at the top of each page. They give you the first and last names on the page.

Suppose you want to find Mary Renn's phone number. You know her father's name is David. You look up David Renn's number in the phone book. Can you find the number on the sample page above?

Knowing your friend's address may also be helpful. Suppose you want to call Peter Reeves. You know he lives on Euclid Avenue. Can you find his number?

Follow these guides when you use the phone book.

Guides for Using the Phone Book

1. Open the book to the first letter of your friend's last name.

2. Look for the guide words that come before and after your friend's last name.

3. Find your friend's last name.

4. Look for the name of your friend's father or mother

      or

5. Look for the street address of your friend.

6. Copy your friend's number in a notebook or address book.

Exercise Using a Phone Book

For these questions, use the sample page from a phone book. Write the answers to the questions on your paper.

1. What is Karl Renner's address?

2. Suppose Jane Reno moved to town. Where would her name be in the phone book? Which name on the sample page would come right before hers?

3. You want to call a friend named Sandy Reeve. Her father's name is Charles Reeve. She lives on Donald Avenue. What is her phone number?

Part 5 Taking a Message

It's nice when you can do a favor for someone. You can be very helpful to others if you learn to take messages carefully.

Suppose someone asks you to give a message to another friend. You should write down the information. Then check to make sure the message is correct.

Holly went to the store to buy some bread for her mother. There she met her mother's friend, Ms. Beck. Here is their conversation.

MS. BECK: Hello, Holly. How are you?

HOLLY: Hello, Ms. Beck. I'm fine, thank you.

MS. BECK: I've been meaning to call your mother, Holly. Would you give her a message for me?

HOLLY: I'll be glad to. What is it?

MS. BECK: Tell her that I will bring the papers to your house next Thursday afternoon.

HOLLY: I'll be sure to tell her, Ms. Beck. You'll bring the papers to our house next Thursday afternoon.

MS. BECK: That's right, Holly. Thank you.

HOLLY: You're welcome.

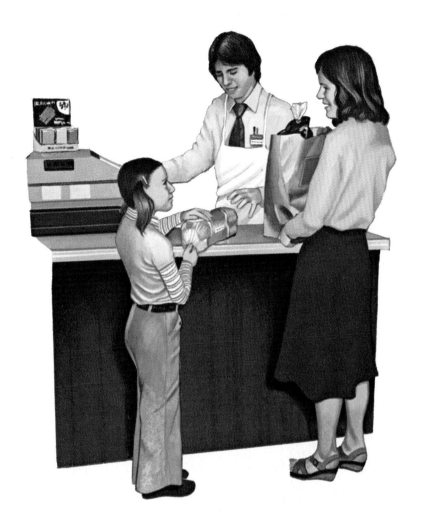

Here is a picture of Holly's message for her mother.

Dear Mom,
    I saw Ms. Beck at the store. She had a message for you. She will bring the papers to our house next Thursday afternoon.
                            Holly

43

Sometimes you need to take a telephone message. Always keep a pencil and paper near the phone. Write the name of the person who should get the message. Then write the message. Let's look at an example.

The telephone rings. Tommy answers it. Tommy is the only one at home.

TOMMY: Hello.

VOICE: Hello. This is Mr. Steel at the service station. May I speak to Mr. Gibson, please?

TOMMY: He can't come to the phone now. May I take a message?

VOICE: Yes, thank you. Mr. Gibson's car is ready to be picked up.

TOMMY: All right, Mr. Steel. I'll tell my father that his car is ready.

VOICE: Thank you. Goodbye.

TOMMY: Goodbye.

When the caller asked to speak to Tommy's father, Tommy said, "He can't come to the phone now."

For safety reasons, it is best not to tell strangers that your parents aren't home. Just take the message politely. Repeat the message to be sure it's right. Then say goodbye and hang up the phone.

Dear Dad,
Mr. Steel called. He said
your car is ready.
Tommy

Guides for Taking a Message

1. Write the name of the person who should get the message.
2. Write the message clearly.
3. Reread the message to check for mistakes.
4. Write your name at the bottom.

Exercises **Taking a Message**

A. Write these messages. Follow the Guides for Taking a Message.

1. You meet your teacher in the drugstore on Saturday morning. She wants you to tell your parents about the P.T.A. meeting. It will be held on Tuesday night at 8:00.

2. Your mother calls you from work. She wants you to remind your sister Sally to go to her dancing lesson. The lesson begins at 4:00.

B. Now you will practice taking telephone messages. Divide into pairs. Take turns calling your partner. The caller should leave a message. The other person will write the message. Follow the Guides for Taking a Message.

Chapter 4

Learning About Sentences

Part 1   What Is a Sentence?

When you talk or write, you use words. Usually, you put your words together in groups. Some of those groups are **sentences.** A **sentence** is a group of words that tells a complete idea.

Here are some examples of sentences.

The boys talk together.

This group of words tells you that there are some boys. It tells you what the boys do. The group of words tells a complete idea. It is a sentence.

47

Kevin has blue slacks.

This group of words tells you that there is a boy named Kevin. It tells you that Kevin has something. It tells what Kevin has. The group of words tells a complete idea. It is a sentence.

This turtle is my pet.

This word group tells you that there is a turtle. It tells what the turtle is. The group of words tells a complete idea. It is a sentence.

Not All Groups of Words Are Sentences

Not all groups of words are sentences. For example, read this word group.

Toni caught.

What did Toni catch? Did she catch a ball? Did she catch a cold? The group of words does not tell you. It does not give a complete idea. It is not a sentence.

A **sentence** is a group of words that tells a complete idea. A sentence tells who or what it is talking about. It tells something about that person or thing.

Word Order

The way you put words together in a sentence is important. We call this word order. Here is a group of words that is not in correct word order.

Games the played children.

That word group makes no sense.

However, we can put the words into the correct order. Then the word group makes sense.

The children played games.

Sometimes the words in a sentence can change places and still make sense. However, the idea of the sentence changes with the word order.

Read this sentence. Make a picture in your mind of the idea it tells.

The paper is on the book.

Now we will change the word order. Read the new sentence.

The book is on the paper.

Did the picture in your mind change? We used the same words in both sentences. However, the different word order changed the meaning.

Exercises Finding Sentences

A. Number your paper from 1 to 10. Read each of the following groups of words. Decide whether each group of words tells a complete idea. If it does, write *Sentence*. If it does not, write *Not a Sentence.*

1. My red sweater.
2. Danny went to the circus.
3. Marcy paints pictures of horses.
4. Walked to school.
5. Chris is my best friend.
6. In the back seat.
7. Cats chase birds.
8. Carla and her sisters.
9. Superman fights crime.
10. Played a good game.

B. The words in each of the sentences below may be put into a different order. Each order will tell a different idea.

Copy each sentence below. Then change some words around to make a different sentence. Use all the same words. Write your new sentences on your paper.

Sample Sentence The cat chased the mouse.
New Order The mouse chased the cat.

1. The hawk saw a rabbit.
2. Jenny called Father.
3. Kenji waited for Lucy.
4. The lost dog found Pat.
5. Nick read to Marnie.
6. Ben splashed water at Sara.

Part 2 Kinds of Sentences

There are four kinds of sentences. Each kind does a different job. This list shows the different kinds of sentences.

> statements
> questions
> commands
> exclamations

When you write a sentence, you must show where it begins. Every sentence begins with a capital letter.

> Many children have gardens.

When you write a sentence, you must also show where it ends. There are three different marks that show that sentences are finished. Here are the three ending marks.

. period
? question mark
! exclamation point

Each kind of sentence has a certain kind of ending mark.

Statement

A statement is a sentence that tells something. It ends with a period.

Billy worked in his garden.
He grew vegetables.

Question

A question is a sentence that asks something. It ends with a question mark.

Are the tomatoes ripe?
Where are the carrots?

Command

A command is a sentence that tells someone to do something. Usually, a command ends with a period.

Please water those flowers.
Take care of your tools.

Exclamation

An exclamation is a sentence that shows strong feeling. It might show excitement, or anger, or fear. It ends with an exclamation point.

What a big bee that is!
How noisy it is!

The four kinds of sentences are statements, questions, commands, and exclamations.

Begin every sentence with a capital letter.

End statements and commands with periods.
End questions with question marks.
End exclamations with exclamation points.

Exercises Telling the Kinds of Sentences

A. This list of sentences has five statements and five commands. Number your paper from 1 to 10. Read each sentence. Then write *Statement* or *Command* to tell what kind of sentence it is.

Sample Sentence Wear your gloves.
Answer Command

1. Close the door.
2. It is cold today.
3. The wind blew down a branch.
4. Watch out for puddles.
5. This toy uses batteries.
6. Don't run into the street.
7. Watch this magic trick.
8. Brian likes bubblegum.
9. Karen waited for the bus.
10. Hang your coat on the hook.

B. This list of ten sentences has six questions and four exclamations. Write each sentence correctly. Use a capital letter at the beginning. Use a question mark at the end of every question. Use an exclamation point at the end of every exclamation.

1. Is your bike new
2. What a great game we saw
3. Where is my cap
4. What time is it
5. How warm the water is
6. What a sunburn you have
7. What is the Big Dipper
8. How sour this milk tastes
9. Are we going to the movie
10. How much do tickets cost

C. This list of sentences has all four kinds mixed together. Write each sentence correctly. Use a capital letter at the beginning of each sentence. Use a period, a question mark, or an exclamation point at the end.

1. today is my birthday
2. i am eight years old
3. will you come to my party
4. we will play games
5. come to my house at noon
6. what a delicious cake this is
7. do you like strawberry ice cream
8. how hot the room is
9. please open the window
10. did you enjoy the party

Part 3 The Parts of the Sentence

Every sentence has two parts. The parts are called the **subject** and the **predicate.**

The Subject

The subject tells *who* or *what* does something. In each of these sentences, the subject has a line under it.

<u>Andrea</u> wins every race.
<u>My best friend Andrea</u> wins every race.
(who)

<u>The tree</u> is falling.
<u>The tallest tree in the park</u> is falling.
(what)

A subject may have one word or more than one word. Read the subjects in the sample sentences again. Count the underlined words in each sentence.

The Predicate

The predicate tells what the subject does. It may tell what the subject is. It may also tell what the subject has.

In each of these sentences, the predicate has two lines under it.

The baby <u>cries</u>.
The baby <u>cries for its bottle</u>.
  (what the subject does)

The clown <u>is</u> funny.
The clown <u>is the funniest person in the circus</u>.
  (what the subject is)

Kunja <u>has</u> sneakers.
Kunja <u>has new blue sneakers with white laces</u>.
  (what the subject has)

A predicate may have one word or more than one word. Read the predicates in the sample sentences again. Count the underlined words in each sentence.

The **subject** of a sentence tells who or what does something.

The **predicate** of a sentence usually tells what the subject does. Sometimes it tells what the subject is. Sometimes it tells what the subject *has*.

Every sentence must have a subject and a predicate.

Exercises   Working with Subjects and Predicates

A. Think of a predicate for each of the following subjects. Write a complete sentence using each subject.

1. the elephant
2. our team
3. the robot
4. the fire engine
5. the squirrel
6. our teacher
7. the hero
8. the kitten
9. my brother
10. Ann

B. Think of a subject for each of the following predicates. Write a complete sentence using each predicate.

1. won the race
2. watched TV
3. laughed
4. sounds too loud
5. played the piano
6. is hot
7. climbs trees
8. came from outer space
9. dried the dishes
10. is always hungry

C. Copy each of the following sentences. Draw one line under the subject of each sentence. Draw two lines under the predicate.

1. The spaceship landed.
2. Henry is my brother.
3. Meg went on a trip.
4. Juan ran home.
5. Sandy plays baseball.
6. Our class visited the zoo.
7. Summer is my favorite season.
8. My mother bought a car.
9. This soup is too hot.
10. Ken carried his baby sister.

More Exercises

Learning About Sentences

A. Finding Sentences   (Use after page 49.)

Number your paper from 1 to 10. Read each of the following groups of words. Decide whether each group of words tells a complete thought. If it does, write *S*. If it does not, write *N. S.*

1. On a sunny day.
2. Carmen fed the gerbil.
3. Plays the trumpet.
4. The stars twinkle.
5. The lamb and its mother.
6. The earth moves around the sun.
7. Bears live in the forest.
8. Bees around the honeycomb.
9. The rose bush in the garden.
10. Jerry mows the lawn.

B. Telling the Kinds of Sentences   (Use after page 53.)

This list of sentences has all four kinds mixed together. Write each sentence correctly. Use a capital letter at the beginning of each sentence. Use a period, a question mark, or an exclamation point at the end.

1. my name is Sheila
2. who is making that noise
3. close the window
4. what a big dog that is

5. will you carry this box
6. Jack has a toothache
7. smoke is coming from the wastebasket
8. wear your raincoat
9. when does the show begin
10. ants carry heavy loads

C. Working with Subjects and Predicates
(Use after page 56.)

Copy each of the following sentences. Draw one line under the subject of each sentence. Draw two lines under the predicate.

1. This barn holds fifty cows.
2. The dragon blew fire.
3. The caboose came last.
4. Thunderstorms scare me.
5. Tigger jumped on Rabbit.
6. Susan and Leah are friends.
7. Maple leaves turn red and yellow.
8. The caterpillar spun a cocoon.
9. The firefighters grabbed the hose.
10. The Indians danced around the fire.

Chapter 5

Learning About Nouns

Our language has thousands of words. It has words for people. It has words for places. It has words for things. It even has words for ideas.

You already know and use hundreds of these words. You learn new ones almost every day.

In this book, you will study five different groups of words. This chapter tells about one large group of words called nouns.

Part 1 What Are Nouns?

You are a student. You are at school. You are reading a book.

Student is a word that names you. *School* is a word that names the place where you are. *Book* is a word that names the thing you are reading. *Student, school,* and *book* are all **nouns.** Nouns are names of persons, places, and things.

> A **noun** is a word that names a person, place, or thing.

Everything you see has a name. These names are nouns. Here are some nouns that name persons, places, or things you can see.

grass	dentist	Madeline	cheese
sky	parents	Max	milk
building	baby	Texas	apples
town	students	Atlanta	bread

Name two other persons or things that you can see. These words are nouns.

Nouns also name things you hear or feel. Here are some nouns of this kind.

music   voices   wind   warmth

Name two other things you can hear or feel. These words are nouns, too.

Some nouns name things you cannot see or hear or feel. These nouns name ideas. Here are some nouns that name ideas.

> friendship   hope   reasons   fright
> goodness   belief   wishes   love

Name two more ideas. These words are nouns.

Exercises   Finding Nouns

A. Number your paper from 1 to 10. Find the nouns in the following sentences. Write the nouns on your paper.

1. The bus stops at my street.
2. This store sells boots and shoes.
3. Ronald is known for his politeness.
4. The dog barked during the night.
5. Marcia made a wish on a star.
6. Boston is a busy city.
7. Most planes land on runways.
8. My grandmother lives in Texas.
9. James found a dime.
10. The tiny cars sped on the racetrack.

B. On your paper, make lists of nouns according to these directions.

1. Names of four vegetables
2. Names of four kinds of animals
3. Names of four pieces of furniture
4. Names of four kinds of flowers.

Part 2 Common Nouns and Proper Nouns

One kind of noun names any person, place, or thing in a large group of persons, places, or things. For example, *street* is a name for any street anywhere. *Pet* is a name for any animal that belongs to anyone. We call nouns like *street* and *pet* **common nouns.**

> A **common noun** names a whole group of persons, places, or things.

Another kind of noun names a particular person, place, or thing. *Mulberry Street* is the name of a particular street. *Willie* is the name of a particular dog belonging to a certain child. We call nouns like *Mulberry Street* and *Willie* **proper nouns.**

> A **proper noun** names a particular person, place, or thing.

Your name is special to you. When you write it, you show that it is special. You begin it with a capital letter.

Every proper noun is the name of a certain person, place, or thing, so it is special too. When you write a proper noun, you show that it is a special name. You begin it with a capital letter.

Often a proper noun has more than one word. You begin every important word in the noun with a a capital letter. Here are some examples of proper nouns. Notice how capital letters are used.

Kim Lee	Monday	Mr. Adams
Ohio	February	Raymond
Cheerios	Thanksgiving	Salt Lake City

Capital letters are not used for little words like *in, of,* and *the* in a proper noun.

Jack <u>in</u> <u>the</u> Box Restaurant   Fourth <u>of</u> July

Also, capital letters are not used for *a, an,* or *the* before a proper noun.

<u>an</u> Arby's Restaurant   <u>the</u> Fourth of July

> Begin every important word of a proper noun with a capital letter.

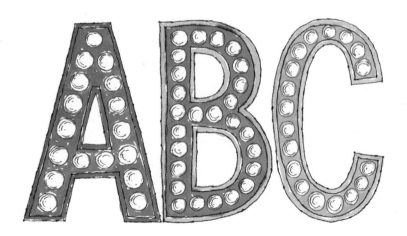

65

Exercises   Finding Common Nouns and Proper Nouns

A. Number your paper from 1 to 10. Find the proper nouns in the following sentences. Write the proper nouns on your paper. Remember to use capital letters.

1. Georgia pulled a wagon down the street.
2. Columbus discovered America in 1492.
3. This letter came from California.
4. Brazil is a country in South America.
5. Maria moved here from New York City.
6. Mount Everest is the highest mountain in the world.
7. My new teacher is Mrs. Ferguson.
8. Kim camped at Yellowstone National Park.
9. My piano teacher lives on Fifth Street.
10. The Lincoln Memorial is a building in Washington, D.C.

B. Number your paper from 1 to 12. Copy each of the following nouns. If the noun is a proper noun, change its first letter to a capital letter.

1. mars
2. planet
3. october
4. school
5. florida
6. president adams
7. refrigerator
8. africa
9. dr. franklin
10. river
11. clark kent
12. susan

common noun—the monument
proper noun—the Washington Monument

Part 3 Singular Nouns and Plural Nouns

The noun *apple* names one apple. If you want to talk about more than one apple, you must change the noun *apple* to *apples*. *Apples* means more than one.

Apple is a singular noun. A **singular noun** names one person, place, or thing.

Apples is a plural noun. A **plural noun** names more than one person, place, or thing.

Most nouns are like *apple*. They change their form to show when they are plural. Usually, plural nouns have an *-s* ending.

> *birds* means more than one *bird*
> *feathers* means more than one *feather*
> *nests* means more than one *nest*

However, some nouns change their forms in other ways. For example, the singular noun *child* changes to the plural noun *children*.

Here are the most common ways to change singular nouns to plural nouns:

1. To form the plural of most singular nouns, add s.

fruit<u>s</u>   vegetable<u>s</u>   meat<u>s</u>   food<u>s</u>

2. When the singular noun ends with the following letters, add *es:*

s	loss<u>es</u>	bus<u>es</u>
sh	bush<u>es</u>	dish<u>es</u>
ch	sandwich<u>es</u>	bunch<u>es</u>
x	fox<u>es</u>	ax<u>es</u>

3. When the singular noun ends in a consonant and *y,* change the *y* to *i* and add *es.*

penny—penn<u>ies</u>   hobby—hobb<u>ies</u>   fly—fl<u>ies</u>

4. Some singular nouns form their plurals in special ways.

man—men   woman—women   child—children
foot—feet   tooth—teeth   mouse—mice

Exercises   Forming Plural Nouns

A. Number your paper from 1 to 12. Copy the following nouns. After each singular noun, write *s*. After each plural noun, write *pl.*

1. chairs	5. church	9. foot
2. cookies	6. mice	10. flower
3. story	7. pencil	11. wishes
4. branches	8. boxes	12. pennies

B. Copy the following singular nouns. After each noun, write the plural of that noun.

1. boy	5. school	9. berry
2. fox	6. child	10. tooth
3. woman	7. party	11. brush
4. sandwich	8. house	12. pony

Part 4 Making Nouns Show Possession

You have seen that the form of a noun tells something about that noun. Nouns may be common or proper. A capital letter at the beginning of a noun usually shows it is a proper noun. Nouns may be singular or plural. An *-s* or *-es* at the end of a noun usually shows it is a plural noun.

There is one other special form for nouns. This special form shows when a noun owns or possesses something. It is called a **possessive form** of a noun.

Here are some pairs of nouns. In each pair, the first noun is a possessive noun. The second noun tells what belongs to the person named by the first noun.

Karen's bike	the teacher's desk
Tony's gloves	the child's voice

> A **possessive noun** is a noun that shows ownership or possession.

Look at the ending of each of the possessive nouns in the examples. The mark you see is an **apostrophe.**

Each of the possessive nouns in the examples above is a singular noun. To make a singular noun show possession, you add an apostrophe and an *s.*

69

Karen's	teacher's
Tony's	child's

Here are some other pairs of nouns. Again, the first noun in each pair is a possessive noun. However, each of these nouns is a plural possessive noun. Notice how the possessive ending is different.

the girls' bikes   the teachers' desks
the boys' gloves   the dogs' collars

Each of these plural nouns already has an *s*. It is difficult to say a word with two *s* endings. Therefore, each plural noun that ends in *s* adds only an apostrophe to show possession.

girls'   teachers'
boys'   dogs'

Some plural nouns do not end in *s*. These plural nouns add an apostrophe and an *s* to show possession.

the children**'s** game   the mice**'s** nest

> A singular noun shows possession by adding an apostrophe and an *s*.
>
> A plural noun that ends in *s* shows possession by adding only an apostrophe.
>
> A plural noun that does not end in *s* shows possession by adding an apostrophe and an *s*.

the dogs' collars

the children's game

Exercises Making Nouns Show Possession

A. Copy each underlined noun. Change each one to show possession. You will add an apostrophe and an *s* to some of them. To others, you will add only an apostrophe.

1. <u>David</u> dog shakes hands.
2. The <u>blackbirds</u> cries are loud.
3. The <u>mice</u> nest is under the porch.
4. The <u>doctor</u> office is nearby.
5. Barbara joined the <u>girls</u> game.
6. We listened to the <u>coach</u> directions.
7. The <u>winners</u> prizes are valuable.
8. Sarah climbed into the <u>engineer</u> seat.
9. The dentist cleaned <u>Hector</u> teeth.
10. Both <u>cats</u> tails are black.

B. Copy the following sentences. Make the underlined nouns show possession.

1. The <u>children</u> teacher left the room.
2. The <u>baby</u> rattle fell.
3. The <u>twins</u> birthday is today.
4. The <u>carpenter</u> tools are in the box.
5. My <u>family</u> house is blue.
6. Judy called her <u>friend</u> name.
7. The <u>players</u> uniforms are muddy.
8. We visited <u>Grandmother</u> apartment.
9. The <u>ducks</u> pond freezes in winter.
10. <u>Eric</u> jokes are funny.

71

More Exercises

Learning About Nouns

A. Finding Nouns   (Use after page 63.)

Number your paper from 1 to 10. Find the nouns in the
following sentences. Write the nouns on your paper.

1. The cocoa burned my tongue.
2. Miguel collects colorful rocks.
3. Rita planted tulips in her garden.
4. My dog can catch a Frisbee.
5. The concert was held in the gym.
6. The cereal is on the top shelf.
7. Carol watches cartoons on TV.
8. The writer made up stories about the future.
9. Alex and his family had a picnic in the park.
10. Raccoons sometimes sleep in hollow logs.

B. Finding Common Nouns and Proper Nouns
   (Use after page 65.)

Number your paper from 1 to 10. Find the proper nouns
in the following sentences. Write the proper nouns on
your paper. Remember to use capital letters.

1. Aunt Betty invited us for supper.
2. The Good Books Club meets every Tuesday.
3. The spaceship circled Jupiter.
4. General Grant fought in the Civil War.
5. My birthday is in January.
6. Mexico lies to the south of the United States.

7. The New York Yankees will play our team.
8. Mom read us a book by Dr. Seuss.
9. Marta climbed to the top of the tree.
10. The ice cream store is on Noble Road.

C. Forming Plural Nouns   (Use after page 68.)

Copy the following singular nouns. After each noun, write the plural form of that noun.

1. dog   5. kitten   9. puppy
2. home   6. foot   10. match
3. dish   7. copy   11. man
4. fairy   8. monster   12. mouse

D. Making Nouns Show Possession   (Use after page 70.)

Copy the underlined noun in each sentence. Change each one to show possession. You will have to add an apostrophe and an s to some of them. To others, you will add only an apostrophe.

1. The scissors are on Pat desk.
2. Charlie Brown filled Snoopy dish.
3. The boys boots are in the hall.
4. The wind knocked down the bird nest.
5. I like that singer voice.
6. The clowns cars are tiny.
7. Mom and Dad painted my brothers bedroom.
8. The nurses uniforms are clean and white.
9. The Indian followed the bear tracks.
10. Nora sister is in first grade.

73

Chapter 6

Learning About Pronouns

Part 1 What Are Pronouns?

You have learned about one large group of words, called nouns. Nouns are words that name persons, places, or things. Find the nouns in this sentence.

Betsy climbed the bars.

Did you find *Betsy* and *bars?* Betsy is a proper noun. It names a person. *Bars* is a common noun. It names a thing.

Now see how the sentence is changed.

She climbed the bars.

The word *she* is used in place of *Betsy*. *She* stands for a person. However, the word *she* does not name the person. *She* is not a noun. *She* stands for a noun.

Here is another way the sentence may be changed.

She climbed *them.*

What new word took the place of *bars? Them* stands for a thing. However, the word *them* does not name the thing. *Them* is not a noun. *Them* stands for a noun.

She and *them* are pronouns. **Pronouns** are words that stand for nouns. Some pronouns stand for singular nouns. Other pronouns stand for plural nouns. Here are some important pronouns.

	Singular	Plural
These are pronouns you use to talk about yourself.	I, me	we, us
These are pronouns you use to talk about the person you are speaking to.	you	you
These are pronouns you use to talk about other persons or things.	he, him she, her it	they, them

Exercises Finding Pronouns

A. Copy the following sentences. Underline the pronouns.

1. I told her a secret.
2. You are all invited.
3. We rode a bus to school.
4. Tell me a story.
5. He made a touchdown.
6. The talking robot surprised them.
7. Can you find the North Star?
8. She is Tammy's best friend.
9. The scream made us shiver.
10. Ed will take him for a walk.

B. Number your paper from 1 to 10. Write every pronoun used in the following sentences. After each pronoun, write the noun or nouns it stands for.

1. Vera was late. Maria waited for her.
2. Bob lost a dime. He looked for it.
3. Peter, would you open the window, please?
4. The clock broke. Dad fixed it.
5. Terry and Beth are best friends. They play together.
6. The class went on a trip. We went to the shore.
7. The telephone rang, and Joe answered it.
8. Steve was watching squirrels. He saw them climb the trees.
9. Della picked strawberries. She likes strawberries and cream.
10. Sunshine is good for plants. It helps them grow.

Part 2   Using Pronouns as Subjects

A noun may be used in any place in a sentence. Most pronouns may not. Some pronouns may be used only as the subject of a sentence. Other pronouns may not be used as the subject at all. The pronouns below may be used as subjects of sentences.

I   we   you   he   she   it   they

The sentences below show the correct way to use these pronouns.

I play checkers well.
You are a good player, too.
We can play a game now.
He is learning the game.
She won that time.
It is not a hard game.
They enjoy playing.

Some subjects have two parts. One part may be a pronoun. Here is an example.

Karen and *I* talked.

78   Both parts of the subject may be pronouns. Read this example.

You and *he* may have the next turns.

Sometimes it is difficult to choose the right pronoun. For example, read this sentence. Think of the pronoun that will fill the blank correctly.

> Vincent and _____ (*she* or *her*) played Ping Pong.

There is a good way to find the right pronoun. Take the subject apart. Try the sentence with just one part of the subject at a time.

> Vincent played Ping Pong.
> _____ (*She* or *Her*) played Ping Pong.

Now the sentence is less confusing. You can see that the pronoun is in the subject. The pronoun *she* may be used as a subject. The right pronoun for the sentence is *she*.

> *She* played Ping Pong.
> Vincent and *she* played Ping Pong.

These pronouns may be used as subjects of sentences.

I   we   you   he   she   it   they

Exercises   Using Pronouns as Subjects

A. In each of these sentences, the subject is a noun. Find the subject. Change the subject to a pronoun. Write your new sentence.

> Sample Sentence The phone rang.
> New Sentence It rang.

1. James sings well.
2. The movie lasted for two hours.
3. The children are ready.
4. Mrs. Johnson drove us to the meeting.
5. Thomas Jefferson was a clever man.
6. The cat played with the ball of yarn.
7. The girls played catch.
8. Ms. Lopez gave us our change.
9. Superman soared over the city.
10. The robot rolled up the ramp.

B. Copy the following sentences. Choose the right pronoun.

1. (He, Him) reads the newspaper.
2. (She, Her) is tall.
3. Mom and (I, me) ate soup for lunch.
4. Lily and (them, they) are on the winning team.
5. (We, Us) planned a carnival.
6. John and (him, he) packed the suitcase.
7. Dad and (us, we) drove to the beach.
8. (They, Them) searched for their dog.
9. (Her, She) and Frank marched in the parade.
10. Kumi and (he, him) put up new wallpaper.

Part 3 Using Pronouns in Other Parts of the Sentence

The pronouns *I, we, she, he,* and *they* may be used as subjects only. They may not be used anywhere else in a sentence. There are other pronouns that may not be used as subjects. However, they may be used in any other part of the sentence. The pronouns in the following list may be used anywhere except as the subject.

me   us   him   her   them

It and *you* may be used anywhere in a sentence.

The following sentences show some correct ways to use *me, us, him, her,* and *them.*

> Look at *me.*
> Roberto gave the ball to *us.*
> The letter for *him* is on the table.
> Grandmother asked *her* a question.
> Laura called *them* to dinner.

These pronouns may not be used as subjects of sentences.
me   us   him   her   them
They may be used anywhere else in a sentence.

These pronouns may be used anywhere in a sentence.
it   you

Exercises   Using Pronouns in Other Parts
of the Sentence

A. In each of these sentences, one or more words are underlined. Use a pronoun in place of the underlined word or words. Write your new sentence.

> Sample Sentence   Mark raked the leaves.
> New Sentence   Mark raked them.

1. Would you please feed the turtle?
2. Jay played checkers with his sister.
3. The librarian read the story to our class.
4. Mom made hot cereal for Danny.
5. The vendor sold hot dogs to Dad and me.
6. I can see the garden from my window.
7. Go and sit by Charles.
8. Denise rode the Twister with Val and Carl.
9. Try the magic trick with Anna.
10. The bus driver stopped for Jim and Alice.

B. Copy the following sentences. Choose the right pronoun.

1. Heather made a gift for (he, him).
2. The coat is too big for (she, her).
3. The judges gave the prize to (they, them).
4. The teacher read a story to (we, us).
5. Manuel explained the rules to Roger and (I, me).
6. I shared my snack with Pam and (he, him).
7. Dad bought tickets for (she, her) and Nancy.
8. Penny asked Tom and (we, us) a question.

Part 4 Possessive Pronouns

You have learned that nouns can show ownership. A possessive noun has a special ending to show ownership. That ending is an apostrophe, or an apostrophe and an *s*. Here are some pairs of nouns. The possessive nouns are underlined. Find the endings on the possessive nouns that show ownership.

Mother's job   the boys' gloves

Pronouns can show ownership, too. However, possessive pronouns do not have endings with apostrophes. Possessive pronouns are special forms of pronouns.

Here are some pairs of words. The possessive pronouns are underlined.

her job   their gloves

In the examples above, the pronouns *her* and *their* are used with nouns. There are also possessive pronouns that may be used by themselves. Here are some examples of both kinds of possessive pronouns.

With Nouns	Alone
Our bus is late.	The late bus is *ours*.
Her coat was red.	The red coat was *hers*.
My pencil is sharp.	The sharp pencil is *mine*.

Study the chart on the following page. It shows the pronouns you use the most.

Pronouns Used as Subjects	Pronouns Used in Other Parts of Sentences	Possessive Pronouns Used with a Noun	Used Alone
I	me	my	mine
we	us	our	ours
you	you	your	yours
he	him	his	his
she	her	her	hers
it	it	its	its
they	them	their	theirs

Exercise   Using Possessive Pronouns

Each of these sentences has one or more underlined words. Use a possessive pronoun in place of the underlined word or words. Write your new sentence.

Sample Sentence 1   Margie is <u>Larry's</u> sister.
Answer 1   Margie is his sister.
Sample Sentence 2   That coat is <u>Jean's coat</u>.
Answer 2   That coat is hers.

1. That sweater is <u>my sweater</u>.
2. Ramsey is <u>Rochelle's</u> dog.
3. Is this <u>your ball</u>?
4. The gray house is <u>Phillip's house</u>.
5. Debbie, take <u>Debbie's</u> umbrella today.
6. Those skates are <u>the boys' skates</u>.
7. The red wagon is <u>Joan's wagon</u>.
8. That game is <u>your game</u>.
9. The babysitter made the <u>children's lunch</u>.
10. Miss Anderson is <u>Sandra's</u> teacher.

Part 5 Using Certain Pronouns Correctly

I and *Me*

Whenever you talk about yourself and another person, name yourself last. When you name yourself in the subject of a sentence, use *I*.

Jill and I read that book.

When you name yourself elsewhere in the sentence, use *me*.

Tony gave the book to Jill and me.

Its and *It's*

The possessive pronoun *its* looks very much like the word *it's*. *It's* has an apostrophe. The apostrophe shows there is something missing. *It's* stands for *it is* or *it has*. The following sentences show correct ways to use *it's*.

The TV set is old. *It's* broken. (It is)
We are all tired. *It's* been a long day. (It has)

The possessive pronoun *its* does not have an apostrophe. *Its* means "belonging to it." These sentences show correct ways to use *its*.

The dog hurt *its* paw. (The paw belongs to it.)
Its paw is sore.

Exercises   Using Certain Pronouns Correctly

A. In each sentence, choose the correct words. Write the whole sentence on your paper.

1. (Trisha and I, I and Trisha) raced home.
2. (My sister and I, I and my sister) had a pillow fight.
3. Dad gave a sandwich to (Greg and me, me and Greg).
4. (My class and I, I and my class) went on a trip.
5. Uncle Albert sent a big box to (my brother and me, me and my brother).
6. (I and Ramon, Ramon and I) made breakfast.
7. (Charlotte and I, I and Charlotte) found shells at the beach.
8. Connie came with (me and Sam, Sam and me).
9. (I and Nan, Nan and I) washed the windows.
10. Tracy sat near (me and Ed, Ed and me).

B. Number your paper from 1 to 8. Choose the correct word, either *its* or *it's*. Write the correct word on your paper.

1. (It's, Its) raining today.
2. The wheelbarrow fell on (its, it's) side.
3. My birthday is special. (It's, Its) the first day of spring.
4. The goldfish swam in (it's, its) bowl.
5. The robin has a worm in (its, it's) beak.
6. (Its, It's) my turn to read now.
7. The water lost (it's, its) sparkle.
8. (It's, Its) getting too dark to play.

More Exercises

Learning About Pronouns

A. Finding Pronouns   (Use after page 76.)

Number your paper from 1 to 10. Write every pronoun used in the following sentences. After each pronoun, write the noun or nouns it stands for.

1. The cat licks its paws.
2. The lion tamer gave orders, and the lions obeyed him.
3. Sally raked the leaves. She did a good job.
4. Did you bring your jacks, Lisa?
5. Kevin loves winter. It is his favorite season.
6. Amy and Gretchen were outside. Mother called them in.
7. Brad tied his shoe.
8. Curtis saw the play. He thought it was spooky.
9. The eagle flapped its wings.
10. Andy and Jeff went to the game. They cheered for their team.

B. Using Pronouns as Subjects   (Use after page 79.)

Copy the following sentences. Choose the right pronoun.

1. (She, Her) wants a pet.
2. (Them, They) sold lemonade.
3. (We, Us) lay on the beach.
4. Kitty and (him, he) have skateboards.
5. Carol and (I, me) are thirsty.

6. Peggy and (they, them) played kickball.

7. You and (her, she) should come to the party.

8. George and (they, them) swim in the pool.

9. My cousins and (us, we) went camping together.

10. (He, Him) and (she, her) both have red hair.

C. Using Pronouns in Other Parts of the Sentence
(Use after page 81.)

Copy the following sentences. Choose the right pronoun.

1. Our neighbors waved to (we, us).

2. Would you help (her, she)?

3. A fish just swam past (I, me).

4. Did you go to the movie with Linda and (they, them)?

5. Those pants are too short for (he, him).

6. Take this message to (she, her).

7. Our cat came with Len and (we, us).

8. The game was easy for (her, she) and him.

9. Will you read a story to Theresa and (I, me)?

10. Tomoko will·sit next to Meg and (she, her).

D. Using Possessive Pronouns   (Use after page 84.)

Each of these sentences has one or more underlined words. Use a possessive pronoun in place of the underlined word or words. Write your new sentence.

1. Is this scarf your scarf?

2. Jane's prize is a blue ribbon.

3. That award is Ted's award.

4. The garden is <u>Rick and Kathy's garden</u>.
5. Leo's shoes look like <u>my</u> shoes.
6. The treasure is <u>yours and mine</u>.
7. Miss Evans showed us <u>the snake's</u> skin.
8. <u>Mary and Peter's</u> farm has chickens.
9. This money is <u>Carlotta's money</u>.
10. Alice is <u>Matthew's</u> cat.

E. Using Certain Pronouns Correctly
    (Use after page 85.)

Number your paper from 1 to 10. Choose the correct word, or group of words. Write the correct word, or group of words, on your paper.

1. (I and David, David and I) both read that book.
2. (It's, Its) too hot to sleep.
3. The wind blew with all (its, it's) strength.
4. Mom bought tickets for (me and Angela, Angela and me).
5. (Chico and I, I and Chico) were partners.
6. The house shook. (It's, Its) windows rattled.
7. (Its, It's) almost time for lunch.
8. (Mike and I, I and Mike) played in his room.
9. Put everything back in (it's, its) place.
10. (Misako and I, I and Misako) went swimming.

Chapter 7

Writing Paragraphs

In Chapter 1 you studied words. You learned about many different kinds of words. In Chapter 4 you studied sentences. You learned how to put groups of words together to make sentences.

A sentence is one way of telling something. A paragraph is another way. In this chapter you will study paragraphs. You will learn the answers to these questions.

1. What is a paragraph?
2. What is a topic sentence?
3. How do you write a paragraph?

Part 1 What Is a Paragraph?

A paragraph is a group of sentences. Here is a paragraph.

Freddy Dissel had two problems. One was his older brother Mike. The other was his younger sister Ellen. Freddy thought a lot about being the one in the middle. There was nothing he could do about it. He felt like the peanut butter part of a sandwich, squeezed between Mike and Ellen.

The paragraph has six sentences.

1. Freddy Dissel had two problems.
2. One was his older brother Mike.
3. The other was his younger sister Ellen.
4. Freddy thought a lot about being the one in the middle.
5. There was nothing he could do about it.
6. He felt like the peanut butter part of a sandwich, squeezed between Mike and Ellen.

Each sentence tells a whole thought. Each begins with a capital letter. Each ends with a period.

Look at the first line of the paragraph. It does not start in the same place as the others. It is *indented*. It begins a few spaces to the right.

> A paragraph is a group of sentences.

Exercise   Writing Sentences as a Paragraph

Write these sentences as a paragraph. Remember to indent the first line.

1. There once lived a boy who loved broccoli.
2. He ate broccoli bread, broccoli cakes, and peanut butter and broccoli sandwiches.
3. He munched on broccoli cookies.
4. He drank big glasses of broccoli juice.
5. He even called himself Broc O'Lee.

One Idea

A paragraph explains one idea. It is called the **main idea.** Here is a paragraph. What is the main idea?

> Mr. Sito was very, very old. He was much, much older than I am. He was much older than my mother and father. He was much older than all my aunts and uncles. He was even a little bit older than the white-haired bakery-man down the block.   —JOAN FASSLER

The paragraph is about Mr. Sito's age. This is the main idea.

Here is another paragraph.

> My cat Barney died last Friday. I was very sad. I cried, and I didn't watch television. I cried, and I didn't eat my chicken or even the chocolate pudding. I went to bed, and I cried.
>
> —JUDITH VIORST

What is the main idea of this paragraph?

94

A paragraph explains one idea.

Exercise Choosing the Main Idea

Read each paragraph. Then write the number of the main idea.

Paragraph A

Do you know what the most beautiful bird in the world looks like? Well, when this bird sings, his wings are as blue as the sky. His tail is as gold as the rays of the sun. When he soars above the water, his wings spread out like a rainbow. His body changes colors like a shadow on the sea.

—RENÉE KAROL WEISS

1. what birds eat
2. what a beautiful bird looks like
3. taking pictures of birds

Paragraph B

I am a giant. I wake up in the morning and stretch. My hand almost goes through the ceiling. I brush my teeth with a big broom. I eat ten eggs and drink the juice of fifty oranges. Then I take a whole loaf of bread and butter it down the side. I eat it in two gulps because I am a giant.   —IVAN SHERMAN

1. having a giant for a friend
2. the giant's castle
3. what the giant does in the morning

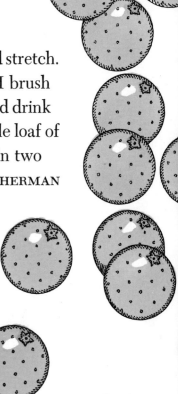

Part 2   The Topic Sentence

A paragraph explains one idea. That idea is given in one sentence. It is called the **topic sentence.** It is usually the first sentence in a paragraph.

Here is a topic sentence. It gives the main idea of the paragraph.

The crickets and the frogs began a musical battle.

Here is the rest of the paragraph. It tells more about the battle.

They wanted to see which could sing the loudest. It was a noisy battle. First the crickets sang out into the night. Then the frogs began. Each one wanted the most silent part of the night for his song.

—GABRIELA MISTRAL

Here is another paragraph. The topic sentence is underlined.

Charles dreamed about taking pictures with his camera. He took a picture of a cat. He took a picture of a tree. He took a picture of the moon. He took a picture of telephone poles from the window of a speeding car. He took a picture of a rose garden.

—MANUS PINKWATER

The paragraph is about Charles's dream of taking pictures with his camera. The topic sentence gives this idea.

> A topic sentence gives the main idea
> of a paragraph.

Exercise   Studying Topic Sentences

Read each paragraph. Then answer the two questions.

Paragraph A

Long ago, African parents taught their children the things they needed to know. The father taught his sons to build the home and to make tools. The mother taught her daughters to grind corn and to cook. She taught both daughters and sons to help care for the younger children.

—MURIEL FEELINGS

1. What is the topic sentence?
2. What is the paragraph about?

Paragraph B

The sea was Maria's only playmate. It talked with Maria. At night it sang her to sleep. It sent its waves along the shore to play games with her. It brought her presents of shells. It gave her the sandy beach all for her own.

—ELIZABETH COATSWORTH

1. What is the paragraph about?
2. What is the topic sentence?

Writing Topic Sentences

You have studied topic sentences. Now you will learn to write them. Here are four steps to follow.

Step 1 Think About a Topic

First, decide what you will write about. Will you write about your uncle's good cooking? your lucky hat? what it feels like to have chicken pox? Think about what you want to say.

Step 2 Take Notes

Next, list the things you will tell about your topic. One boy named Julio chose "My Lucky Hat" as his topic. He listed the special days when he wore his hat.

the first day of school
tests
the dentist's office

Step 3 Decide on the Main Idea

Study your list of ideas. Decide what your paragraph will be about.

Julio studied his list. He decided that this would be the main idea of his paragraph.

when I wear my lucky hat

Step 4 Write a Topic Sentence

Finally, write your topic sentence. Give the main idea of the paragraph.

Julio wrote this sentence.

I wear my lucky hat on special days.

99

Writing a Topic Sentence

Choose one of these topics. Follow the four steps. Write a topic sentence. Save your notes and your topic sentence.

1. Learning to ride a bike
2. How to answer the telephone
3. A dream
4. A special birthday
5. Buying a turtle
6. My favorite relative
7. An exciting trip
8. My hobby

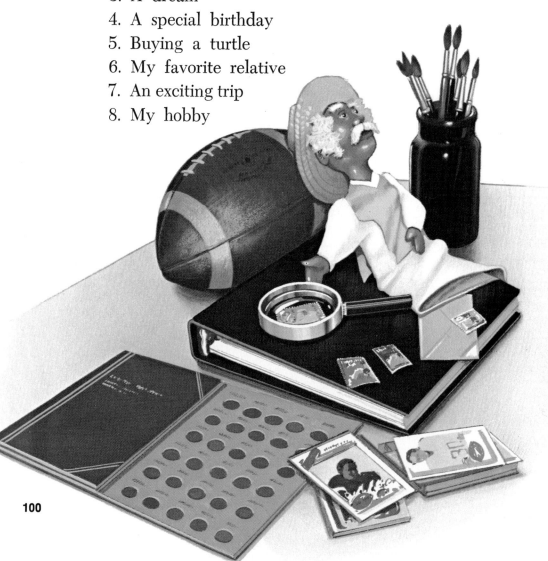

Part 3 Writing a Paragraph

You have learned some important things about paragraphs.

1. A paragraph is a group of sentences.
2. A paragraph explains one idea.
3. A topic sentence gives the main idea of a paragraph.

You have learned how to write a topic sentence. Now you will learn how to write the rest of the paragraph.

Adding Sentences

The topic sentence gives the main idea. The rest of the sentences add to it. They tell more about the main idea. The sentences should be arranged in an order that makes sense.

Here is a paragraph. The topic sentence is underlined.

Young goats are playful animals. They jump high in the air. They chase each other. They play follow-the-leader. They run from morning until night.

The topic sentence tells you that goats are playful. The rest of the sentences tell you how goats play.

1. They jump.
2. They chase each other.
3. They play follow-the-leader.
4. They run.

Here is another paragraph.

1. What is the topic sentence of this paragraph?
2. What is the main idea?

Helena, the Hippopotamus, didn't feel well. She stood all alone in the river and moped. Helena didn't know what to do. She didn't want to eat. She didn't want to swim. She didn't want to play and cool herself in the wet, sticky mud. Poor Helena was very unhappy.   —YUTAKA SUGITA

This is the topic sentence.

Helena, the Hippopotamus, didn't feel well.

What do the rest of the sentences tell about Helena?

The sentences in a paragraph tell about the main idea.

Exercises Writing Paragraphs

A. Follow these directions.

    1. Write this topic sentence on a sheet of paper.

        Sport can do three tricks.

    2. Study the three pictures. Each shows Sport doing one trick.

    3. Write one sentence about each picture. Begin each sentence this way.

        He can _____.

    4. Write all four sentences as a paragraph. Be sure to indent the first line.

B. Take out the notes and the topic sentence you wrote for Part 2.

    1. Copy the topic sentence.

    2. Read the notes.

    3. Write three or four sentences that tell more about the main idea.

    4. Write all the sentences as a paragraph.

103

Chapter 8

Thinking Clearly

Every day you must make decisions. You choose which clothes to wear. You choose answers to questions in class. You decide which friend you want to talk with or play with.

Suppose you must choose one thing to do this afternoon. Your friends want you to play with them. You have a spelling test tomorrow and should study for it. There is a good program on TV, too. How do you decide what to do?

Whenever you make decisions, it is important to think clearly. This chapter will help you know what clear thinking is. It will help you to think clearly.

Part 1 Fact and Opinion

Sometimes when people talk, they give facts. **Facts** are statements that are true. They can be proved. For example, a weather forecaster may say that the temperature is now five degrees below zero.

Other times, people give opinions. **Opinions** are a person's feelings about something. For example, some people may dislike cold weather. Those people will say that the temperature of five degrees below zero is too cold. Other people may like to ski or ice skate. Those people may say that the temperature of five below is just right. Opinions on the same thing are often different from each other.

To think clearly, you must use facts. You should put aside opinions. Think only about the facts in a situation. Then you can decide how to act in that situation.

Suppose you want to get a pet. Your brother says a raccoon would be a good pet. Your sister says a raccoon would be a terrible pet. Which person should you listen to? Should you try to get a raccoon?

First, you must decide whether your brother and sister are giving facts or opinions. In this case, it is easy to decide. You can see that they are giving opinions.

Second, you must find out the facts. You could look up raccoons in an encyclopedia. You might find books about raccoons. You could visit a zoo and look at a live raccoon.

Now you know the facts. You can decide whether a raccoon is a good pet. You can decide whether to try to get one. You have not let others make your decision. You have thought clearly.

Exercises Seeing the Difference between Facts and Opinions

A. In the following list there are six facts. After each fact is an opinion. Think of a different opinion about each fact. Number your paper from 1 to 6. Write your new opinion for each fact.

Sample Fact A jack-o'-lantern is a pumpkin
with a face carved on it.
Sample Opinion Jack-o'-lanterns are scary.
New Opinion Jack-o'-lanterns are fun to make.

Facts	Opinions
1. Potatoes grow underground.	Potatoes taste strange.
2. Many trees lose their leaves in the fall.	Fall is the nicest time of year.
3. The colors yellow and red make orange.	Orange is a pretty color.

4. Birds can fly.   It would be fun to be a bird.

5. Henry Ford made cars.   Ford cars are expensive.

6. Instructors at the Y teach swimming.   Swimming is easy.

B. Here are two lists. In the first list there are six facts. In the second list there are six opinions. Each opinion is about one of the facts. Match each fact with the opinion about that fact. Number your paper from 1 to 6. Write the letter of the opinion after the number of the fact.

Facts

1. Bees have stingers.
2. Sea water is salty.
3. Clouds hold water.
4. *Goggles* is the name of a book.
5. My father is a plumber.
6. This sweater is made of wool.

Opinions

A. Salt is good for you.
B. My father is a good plumber.
C. Clouds are beautiful.
D. Bees are dangerous.
E. This sweater is ugly.
F. The book *Goggles* is easy to read.

Part 2 Generalizations

In Part 1, you learned that you should separate facts from opinions. Sometimes this is not easy. Sometimes opinions sound like facts. You may be tricked into using these opinions in making a decision. Then you will probably make a poor decision. One kind of opinion that may trick you is a generalization.

A **generalization** is a general statement about a whole group of objects or actions. Most often a generalization is unfair.

Here is an example.

Snakes are dangerous.

This generalization seems to be based on facts. Perhaps the speaker has read about some dangerous snakes. The speaker knows some facts about dangerous snakes. But it is unfair to say that snakes in general are dangerous. Not all snakes are dangerous. Here is a better way to make this statement.

Some snakes are dangerous.

The generalization has been changed into a fact.

Here is another example.

That baby always cries.

Can that be true? Can a baby cry *all* the time? A fact may be that the speaker has heard the baby cry often. But *often* does not mean *always*. Here are better ways to say this.

That baby cries often.
I have heard that baby cry many times.

Listening to Commercials

Often people use generalizations to persuade you to do something. Ads on TV or in magazines often use generalizations. The writers are trying to get you to buy something. Here is an example.

Everybody loves Whizzo games.

This statement looks like a fact. But is it? Can *everybody* know about Whizzo games? How can *everybody* love them?

When you read or hear a generalization like that, try to change it into a fact. Here is a statement about Whizzo games that may be a fact.

110

Some people like Whizzo games.

Now it is up to you to decide whether you agree with those people.

Listen to commercials and read ads carefully. Use clear thinking to decide whether to buy things. Look for generalizations. Try to change them into statements that may be true. Then you can better decide whether or not to buy these things.

Exercises Finding Generalizations

A. Number your paper from 1 to 10. Read each of these statements. Some may be true. Others are generalizations and are not true. If the statement may be true, write *Maybe* on your paper. If the statement is a generalization, write *Generalization.*

1. Everybody likes spinach.
2. Some people like spinach.
3. This pair of scissors does not cut well.
4. Scissors are always hard to use.
5. Sun Toothpaste makes teeth sparkle.
6. Some people like to use Sun Toothpaste.
7. Tall people are good at sports.
8. Many good basketball players are tall.
9. Sometimes I feel lazy.
10. Americans are lazy people.

B. To do this exercise, you can listen to radio or TV commercials. You may also read newspaper or magazine ads. Find three generalizations in the commercials or ads. Write down the generalizations. If you can, change each generalization into a statement that may be true. Write your new statements.

Improving Your Speaking and Listening Skills

Most of you like to talk. You talk with your friends or with your parents. You are eager to share your ideas and to express your opinions. You want to talk about your feelings.

You also want people to listen when you talk. Listening is sometimes more important than talking.

To get along well in the world, you need to speak well and to listen carefully. This chapter will help you sharpen your speaking and listening skills.

Part 1 Helping People Listen to You

Often people don't listen. Sometimes this is the speaker's fault. If you are a thoughtful speaker, you will help your listener. You will pronounce your words correctly and clearly. You will not run your sentences together.

Here are some ways to help others listen to you.

Thinking with Your Whole Body

Think hard about what you are saying. Keep thinking. Your actions will follow your thoughts.
Look at the picture below.

Peggy is talking about her new kitten. She is using her hands to show the kitten's size and actions. Her movements help to make clear what she is saying. Her face shows that she is happy to have the kitten.

Peggy is giving clues to her listeners. Her body is almost talking. Her body is saying, "Listen to me. I am telling you about something that is important to me."

Now look at these pictures. What clues are the speakers giving to their listeners? Which speaker seems to be concentrating?

Looking at Your Listeners

Your eyes help you speak. Use them when you talk. Look into your listener's eyes.

Act out each of the following scenes in class. In each one, the speaker does not look into the listener's eyes.

1. Mrs. Wall says hello to Janie. Janie is shy. She looks at her feet and says hello.

2. Kevin is giving a talk about his trip to Disney World. He doesn't look at his listeners. Instead, he stares at the door at the back of the room.

Now talk about the scenes. They show things that happen every day. How do you feel when a speaker doesn't look at you?

Using a Pleasant Voice

You can speak quietly when you talk to one or two people. If you talk to a large group, you will need to speak louder.

When you speak louder, your voice must still be pleasant. If you speak in a complaining tone, no one will listen to you. If you shout, people may turn away.

Take turns. Read the sentences at the top of page 117 aloud. First, speak them in a complaining voice or a shout. Then read the sentences in a pleasant voice. Can you hear the difference?

1. Mom, Jimmy took my ball and glove. He won't give them back.
2. I dusted the erasers yesterday. It's Carol's turn.
3. Juan already had five cookies. He should share the rest of them with us.

Guides for Helping People Listen to You

1. Keep your mind on what you are saying.
2. Speak clearly and distinctly.
3. Let your actions follow your thoughts.
4. Look into your listener's eyes.
5. Make your voice pleasant.

Exercises   Helping People Listen to You

A. What is your favorite wish? Think about it. Write your wish on a piece of paper. Then write three or four sentences that explain your wish.

Sample Wish

I wish I could fly. Every day I would fly to the beach. I could fly over mountains. It would be fun to wave to people in airplanes.

B. After you write your wish, divide into pairs. Say your wish to your partner. Practice saying it several times. You may look at your paper, but try not to read every word.

117

C. Now take turns telling your wish to your class. Follow the Guides for Helping People Listen to You.

Part 2 Reading Aloud

A good reader can make a story come alive. A good listener pays attention to what is being read. Listen now, while your teacher reads "Clouds" to you.

A little mouse went for a walk with his mother. They went to the top of a hill and looked at the sky.

"Look!" said Mother. "We can see pictures in the clouds."

The little mouse and his mother saw many pictures in the clouds. They saw a castle . . .

a rabbit . . .

a mouse.

"I am going to pick flowers," said Mother.

"I will stay here and watch the clouds," said the little mouse.

The little mouse saw a big cloud in the sky. It grew bigger and bigger. The cloud became a cat. The cat came nearer and nearer to the little mouse.

"Help!" shouted the little mouse, and he ran to his mother.

"There is a big cat in the sky!" cried the little mouse. "I am afraid!"

Mother looked up at the sky.

"Do not be afraid," she said. "See, the cat has turned back into a cloud again."

118

The little mouse saw that this was true, and he felt better. He helped his mother pick flowers, but he did not look up at the sky the rest of the afternoon.

—ARNOLD LOBEL

Now read the story to yourself. Think about how you would read it aloud. First of all, you would need to know all the words.

Learning New Words

Before you share a story with others, the words should be easy for you. Look up words you don't know. Practice saying words that are hard.

Here are two words from "Clouds." They may be new to you. Say them out loud. Do you need more practice?

1. castle
2. pictures

Taking Your Time

Don't rush when you read out loud. Give your listeners plenty of time. They need to hear every word. They also need time to think about what is happening in the story.

Be sure to pause when you see a comma or a period.

Picturing What Happens

When you read aloud, use your imagination. In your mind, picture what the words are telling about. For example, imagine the flowers. What colors do you think they are? Could you draw the clouds?

Just for fun, pretend you are going to make a movie of this story. Decide what pictures to take.

Showing Feelings

When you read, make the words come alive. Speak clearly so that people will understand what you say. Try to express the feelings behind the words, too.

Little Mouse gets more and more scared as the cloud grows larger. Imagine that you are Little Mouse watching the cloud. Wouldn't you be frightened, too?

For practice, take turns reading these sentences aloud. Try to show the fear that Little Mouse feels.

The little mouse saw a big cloud in the sky. It grew bigger and bigger. The cloud became a cat. The cat came nearer and nearer to the little mouse.

Making Characters Seem Real

Make the people in your story lively. Follow the clues the author gives you.

Look at another example from "Clouds." Your clue in this sentence is **cried.** How would you read the mouse's words?

"There is a big cat in the sky!" cried the little mouse. "I am afraid."

Now think about Mother Mouse. She seems very calm. She is able to make her son feel better. Take turns reading the following sentences. Try to show how Mother Mouse feels.

"Do not be afraid," she said. "See, the cat has turned back into a cloud again."

Now you are ready to read the whole story out loud. The guides on the following page will help you remember what to do.

Exercises Reading Aloud

A. Read these sentences silently. Think about them. Then take turns reading them aloud. Show feeling.

1. Slowly, the snake wriggled through the grass. It came closer and closer. I couldn't move.

2. What? Did you say I won the blue ribbon?

3. "Ha!" she laughed. "You aren't a real monster. You were just trying to fool me!"

4. "Really, Mr. Brown, you must be wrong. My dog is big, but he never bites."

5. Tim lay on the ground where his bicycle had fallen. Molly walked toward him. Suddenly, Tim jumped up. "I'm okay, Molly!" he shouted.

B. Divide into groups of three. Take turns reading "Clouds" aloud. Follow the Guides for Reading Aloud. After you read, ask the other people in your group to tell you how well you read.

C. Find something you would like to share with your class. It may be a poem or part of a story. Practice your reading. Then read aloud to your class. Follow the guides above.

Part 3 Talking About Your Opinion

Some people like pizza. Do you? Why?

When you answer these questions, you are talking about your opinion. People may have different opinions about the same thing.

Thinking About Your Opinion

To have an opinion, you must think. You should know why you have your opinion.

Here is something for you to think about.

Joy has a cat named Tip. She loves Tip very much. Joy and her family will move far away. It will be hard to move with Tip. Joy's parents think Tip should stay with Joy's cousins. The cousins already have two cats. Joy does not want to give Tip away.

Now discuss these questions in class.

1. What do you think Joy should do?
2. Why do you have your opinion?

Finding Facts

You should base your opinion on facts. A fact is true. It can be proved. Before you decide on your opinion, find facts about the question.

Here are three ways to find facts.

1. You will find some kinds of facts in books. For example, suppose you want to know how ants live. You could find out by looking up "Ants" in the encyclopedia.

2. You can also find facts by talking with people. Perhaps Joanie wants to know if her cousins like cats. The best way to find out would be to ask them.

3. Some facts come from your own experience. Suppose you have always lived in Atlanta, Georgia. Your memory is full of facts about Atlanta. You know that the ground is clay. You know that summers are hot.

Presenting Your Opinion

When you have an opinion, state it clearly. Then tell why you have your opinion. Tell your facts.

Now read the example below. The example shows how Carla presents her opinion.

Why Our Class Should Make an Ant Farm

Our class should make an ant farm. Ants work together as a team. We would learn how they dig tunnels. Feeding the ants would be fun. We could bring them tiny pieces of lettuce and bread crumbs. Watching the ants would teach us about another form of life.

Exercises **Talking About Your Opinion**

A. Copy these sentences on your paper. Write *O* next to the ones that are opinions. Write *F* next to the ones that are facts.

1. Some trees lose their leaves in the fall.
2. Parents should not expect children to work.
3. Five people on our block are left-handed.
4. Dogs should stay off the furniture.
5. Los Angeles is a city in California.

B. Plan a short talk to your class. Talk about your opinion. Choose a subject that interests you. Follow the Guides for Talking About Your Opinion.

Here are some ideas. You may choose one of them. You may also think up your own idea.

1. Why We Should Grow Our Own Vegetables
2. Why Children Should Share Bedrooms
3. Why I Am in Favor of Homework
4. Why Our Class Should Present a Play
5. Why I Like My Sister (or Brother)
6. Why We Should Help To Clean Our Neighborhood

Chapter 10

Giving and Following Directions

Directions are important. They teach you how to go somewhere. They may teach you how to do something. To be helpful, directions must be clear. Have you ever caused a mix-up because you gave someone poor directions?

Even with good directions, people sometimes get confused. To follow directions you must read or listen carefully. It is especially important to learn to follow directions about safety.

Part 1 Giving Directions to Others

José wants to go to Tom's house on Saturday morning. Here are the directions Tom gives to him.

1. Go down your street towards the gas station.
2. Turn right at the gas station.
3. Walk three blocks.
4. Turn left onto Ridge Street.
5. My house is the second from the corner. It is on the left side of the street. The front door is red. The number is 205.

Tom's directions are very clear. He has given them step by step.

What special places has Tom named? What important things does he tell?

Guides for Giving Directions to Others

1. Give all the steps.
2. Name special places and give details.
3. Give each step in order.
4. Check the steps to be sure they are right.

Exercises Giving Directions to Others

A. Look at this map of Lawrence School. The map shows Marie and Clara's classroom. It also shows the principal's office.

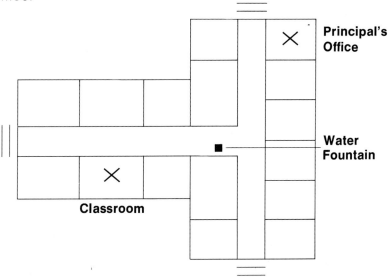

Marie tells Clara how to find the principal's office. This is what she says.

1. Go down the hall.
2. Turn by the water fountain.
3. Go down that hall.
4. The principal's office is next to the stairs.

Clara can't follow the directions. What is wrong with them?

Decide how you would change the directions. Talk about the changes with the rest of your class.

129

B. Write directions from your classroom to the school library. Follow the Guides for Giving Directions to Others.

Part 2 Reading and Following Directions

Directions give you information. Read them carefully. Don't skip any steps. Be careful to follow directions about safety. If you don't understand something, ask for help.

Jenny's Animal Cut-Outs

Jenny's class has been studying wild animals. For her birthday, Jenny's mother gave her a book of stand-up animal pictures to cut out and paste on cardboard squares. These directions came with the set.

1. Cut out each animal.
2. CAUTION: When you cut, always point the scissors away from you.
3. Fold the base of the animal along the dotted line.
4. Glue the base of each animal on the cardboard squares.

Answer these questions. Talk about your answers in class.

Which direction is about safety?

What might happen if Jenny skipped Step 3?

Exercises **Reading and Following Directions**

A. Read these sets of directions. In each example, one step is out of order. Write the steps in the right order.

How To Rake Leaves

1. Get a rake.
2. Rake the leaves into piles.
3. Pull the rake across the ground toward you.

How To Set the Table

1. Place a fork to the left of each plate.
2. Put down a plate for each person.
3. Place a knife to the right of each plate.
4. Put a spoon to the right of each knife.

B. Read the directions below. Copy them on your paper. Underline one step that tells about safety.

How To Change a Light Bulb in a Lamp

1. Unplug the lamp cord.
2. Unscrew the old light bulb.
3. Take out the old light bulb.
4. Screw in a new light bulb.
5. Plug in the lamp cord.

Part 3 Becoming a Careful Listener

Think when someone tells you what to do. If you don't understand, ask questions. Once the directions make sense to you, follow them. Sometimes your good sense tells you that the directions will lead to problems. If this happens, do not follow those directions.

Here is what happened at Cliff's house.

> One day Cliff's older brother John came home from school early. He opened the door, and the cat ran out. The cat climbed a tree. She couldn't get down. She cried loudly.
>
> "Go climb that tree and get the cat, Cliff," said John. "Then bring her to the house. Don't tell anyone she got out. I have to go to Jim's house. I'll see you later."

132

Cliff's parents had told him not to climb trees. Cliff did not think he should follow his brother's directions. What do you think Cliff should have done?

Listening to Emergency Directions

Sometimes you face an emergency. Someone gives you directions. You must listen and act quickly.

Read the scene below. Then answer the questions. Talk about your answers in class.

Fire Alarm

(A loud buzzer sounds in the hall.)

MR. PARK: That's a fire alarm. Stand up. Do not talk. Follow Lee out of class. Leave your books and coats here.

MAX: I'll see you in a minute, Sara. I have to get my jacket.

SARA: Okay, Max. I'll go ahead.

(The students begin moving down the hallway. Max goes back for his jacket.)

MAX: Hey! Where is everyone?

(Max looks around. He runs out the door. He crashes into Paul and Amy.)

AMY: Ow! You stepped on my foot!

PAUL: Stop pushing, Max!

(The buzzer stops. Mr. Walker walks over.)

MR. PARK: It wasn't a real fire this time. You could have been in trouble, Max. You didn't listen when I gave directions.

MAX: What did I do wrong?

1. What mistakes did Max make?
2. What should Sara have done?
3. How did Max put other people's lives in danger?

Guides for Becoming a Careful Listener

1. Think about what you are hearing.
2. Unless there is an emergency, feel free to ask questions.
3. In an emergency, be quiet. Do exactly as you are told.

Exercises Becoming a Careful Listener

Read these questions. Think about your answers. Then talk over your answers in class.

A. Think about things that have happened to you. Have you ever had trouble listening to directions? Tell your story to the class.

B. Suppose someone tells you to come with her in a rowboat. You think the trip might not be safe. What questions would you ask?

C. Here are three sets of directions. What problem do you find in the directions? What changes should be made?

Fixing Cereal for Breakfast

1. Open the cereal box.
2. Pour the milk.
3. Put the cereal in a bowl.

Putting on a Pullover Sweater

1. Slip your arms into the sleeves of the sweater.
2. Pull the sweater over your head.
3. With each hand, hold onto your shirt-sleeve. This will keep your shirt in place when you put on the sweater.

Using a Hammer and Nail

1. Hit the nail with the hammer.
2. Hold the nail steady with one hand.
3. Keep your eyes on the hand holding the nail.

Chapter 11

Learning About Verbs

In Chapter 5 you learned about a group of words called nouns. You learned that there are two kinds of nouns. They are common nouns and proper nouns.

Look at the picture on the opposite page. Can you name any things in the picture with common nouns? Can you name anything with a proper noun?

Chapter 6 told about another group of words called pronouns. Can you change any nouns you used to tell about the picture to pronouns?

In this chapter, you will learn about a third group of words called *verbs*.

Part 1 What Are Verbs?

Imagine you are doing exercises. These sentences tell some of the things you might do.

You stretch.
You bend.
You twist.
You jump.

In each of the sentences, there are only two words. The pronoun *you* is the same in each sentence. *You* names a person. The other words are **verbs.** Each verb tells what the person does. Read the sentences a second time. Make a picture in your mind of each action.

Can you find the verb in each of these sentences?

Peggy climbs trees.
Mike runs races.
Nancy skates.
George swims at the Y.

Each of these verbs tells about an action you can see. You can see someone *climb* trees. You can see someone *run*. You can see someone *skate* or *swim*.

Other verbs tell about actions you cannot see. For example, a person *thinks*. A person *likes* music. A person *wants* friends. *Thinks* and *likes* and *wants* are all verbs. They tell what a person does.

Can you think of another verb of this kind? Your verb must tell what someone does. You must not be able to see the person do it.

Do you remember the two parts of a sentence? Every sentence must have a subject and a predicate. The predicate tells what the subject does. Every predicate must have a verb in it.

Study this chart. Each sentence is divided into subject and predicate. The verb in each predicate is underlined.

Subject	Predicate
Peggy	climbs trees.
Mike	runs races.
Nancy	skates.
George	swims at the Y.
That sign	glows.
I	like music.
Everyone	wants friends.

Notice that some predicates have more than one word. Other predicates have only one word. That one word must be a verb. Every sentence must have a verb.

Exercises Finding Verbs

A. Copy the following sentences. Underline each verb.

> Sample Sentence Rabbits like lettuce.
> Answer Rabbits <u>like</u> lettuce.

1. The kitten purrs.
2. César pulled weeds.
3. Stars twinkle.
4. Rain fell all day.
5. The baby smiled.
6. The painter climbed the ladder.
7. Kirsten threw the ball.
8. The balloon floated away.
9. I see my friend Joan.
10. Arthur waits for the bus here.

B. Copy the following sentences. There is a blank in each sentence. Think of a verb that will fit in that blank. There are several verbs that will fit. Write a verb in each blank.

> Sample Sentence Alice _____ her bike.
> Possible Answer Alice ___fixed___ her bike.

1. I _____ my new sweater.
2. Nicole _____ a good story.
3. The little mouse _____ .
4. The artist _____ a picture.
5. The ape _____ in his cage.
6. Cowboys _____ horses.
7. We _____ a new song.
8. Our team _____ the game.

140

Part 2 Two Kinds of Verbs

Not all verbs do the same job. There are two different kinds of verbs. They do two different jobs. They are action verbs, and verbs that say something is.

Action Verbs

The verbs you learned about in Part 1 are called **action verbs.** Action verbs tell what a person or thing does.

Kim *plays* with her dog.
The balloon *sailed* away.

Some action verbs tell about actions you can see. Others tell about actions you cannot see.

Kim *enjoys* the game.

Exercise   Using Action Verbs

Here are eight groups of words. Change each group into a sentence. Think of an action verb for each group of words. Write your sentence.

Sample Word Group Squirrels trees.
Possible Sentence Squirrels climb trees.

1. Jerry the door.
2. Mice cheese.
3. Fran an apple.
4. A bird its wings.

5. Dentists teeth.
6. Firefighters hoses.
7. Dogs their tails.
8. Pilots planes.

141

Verbs That Say That Something Is

Not all verbs are action verbs. For example, read the following sentences. The verb in each sentence is underlined. None of these verbs tells about action.

The sun <u>is</u> hot.
The crickets <u>are</u> noisy.
I <u>am</u> on the porch.

The first sentence tells about the sun. However, it does not say that the sun does anything. It simply says what the sun is.

The second sentence tells about crickets. It does not say what the crickets are doing. It simply says what the crickets are.

The third sentence tells about the person who is speaking. It does not say what the speaker is doing. It simply says where the speaker is.

Is and *are* and *am* are verbs that tell that something is. They are examples of the second kind of verb.

A **verb** is a word that tells about an action or tells that something is.

There are not many verbs of the second kind. The most important ones are the forms of the verb *be*. You should learn about these forms. The verb *be* is used more than any other verb. If you use its forms correctly, other people will understand you better.

Here are some of the forms of the verb *be*.

am   is   are   was   were

Sometimes you are not sure which form to use. Then think about the subject of your sentence. The right form of the verb depends on the subject. Study the following chart. It shows how to use these forms of *be*.

Subject	Verb	Sample Sentence
I	**am** or **was**	I <u>am</u> early today. I <u>was</u> late yesterday.
you	**are** or **were**	You <u>are</u> tall now. You <u>were</u> short last year.
any other singular noun or pronoun	**is** or **was**	Gloria <u>is</u> my neighbor. She <u>was</u> at my party.
any other plural noun or pronoun	**are** or **were**	The streets <u>are</u> dry now. They <u>were</u> wet this morning.

Exercises   Using Two Kinds of Verbs

A. Number your paper from 1 to 10. Choose the right form of *be*. Write the correct form.

    Sample Sentence Lisa (be, is) late.
    Correct Form of *be* is

1. I (was, be) afraid of the dark.
2. You (is, are) too old for this toy.
3. Karen (am, is) proud of her work.
4. Those boys (is, are) early.
5. My pencils (is, are) sharp.
6. I (am, is) hungry for lunch.
7. The birds (was, were) noisy this morning.
8. We (is, are) happy for you.
9. Sunset (was, were) at 6 o'clock.
10. You (was, were) first in line.

B. Copy each of the following sentences. Some have action verbs. Some have verbs that tell that something is. Underline the verbs.

    Sample Sentence Jonah was here yesterday.
          Answer Jonah <u>was</u> here yesterday.

1. The sun shone brightly.
2. Tom invited me to the party.

3. The tomatoes are ripe.
4. Cheryl opened the window.
5. I am almost nine years old.
6. George Washington was the first president.
7. The children laughed at the clown.
8. You are an honest person.
9. A mason lays bricks.
10. We are ready to go.

C. Some of the following sets of words have verbs. They are sentences. Other sets do not have verbs. They are not sentences. Number your paper from 1 to 10. If the word group has a verb, write *Sentence.* If it does not have a verb, think of a verb that will fit. Write the complete sentence.

Sample Sentence 1 Andy found my jacket.
Answer 1 Sentence

Sample Sentence 2 Judy at the store.
Possible Answers Judy was at the store.
Judy waited at the store.

1. Monkeys on their swings.
2. Kevin combed his hair.
3. Steven funny jokes.
4. Pat piano after school.
5. The bear cub climbed the tree.
6. The police siren loud.
7. My dog knows tricks.
8. Grandmother waved goodbye.
9. Cars down the street.
10. The dentist checked my teeth.

145

Part 3   Using Helping Verbs

You have learned about two kinds of verbs. They are action verbs and verbs that tell that something is.

In this Part you will learn about another group of verbs. These verbs can be used with action verbs. They can also be used with verbs that tell that something is. They are the *helping verbs*.

What Are Helping Verbs?

In many sentences, there is only one word in the verb.

> Bob *talked* with Linda.

In other sentences, there are two, or three, or even four words in the verb.

> Bob *was talking* with Linda.
> Bob *should have talked* with Linda.
> Bob *must have been talking* with Linda.

In these verbs, there is one word that is most important. The most important word is called the **main verb.** Usually, the main verb comes last. All the other words in the verb are called **helping verbs.**

This chart shows the main verbs and the helping verbs in the sample sentences.

Helping Verbs	Main Verbs
was	talking
should have	talked
must have been	talking

There are several helping verbs. However, two groups of helping verbs are the most important. They are the forms of *be* and the verbs *has, have,* and *had.*

Exercise Finding Helping Verbs

Copy the following sentences. In each sentence, underline the main verb and its helping verb.

1. Timmy is playing tag.
2. The roses are blooming.
3. Freddy is reading a book.
4. It was raining all day.
5. Lena has caught three fish.
6. I have heard that poem before.
7. The captain has chosen her team.
8. Paulette has gone to school.
9. The squirrels have eaten the nuts.
10. Dad and Kathy were raking the leaves.

Some Verbs Need Helping Verbs

Some verbs are always used with helping verbs. It is incorrect to use these verbs by themselves.

Sometimes the ending of a verb shows that it needs a helping verb. Usually, verbs that end in *-en* or *-ing* need helping verbs.

eat**en**	I <u>have eaten</u> all the fruit.
driv**en**	My father <u>has driven</u> to Detroit.
sing**ing**	The students <u>were singing</u>.
drink**ing**	Jan <u>is drinking</u> her milk.

There are some verbs that always need helping verbs. Here are four of them.

done	We <u>have done</u> something interesting today.
been	We <u>have been</u> to a picnic.
seen	We <u>have seen</u> our friends.
gone	Now our friends <u>have gone</u> home.

In Chapter 12, you will learn more about verbs that need helping verbs.

Exercises   Using Helping Verbs

A. Find the verb in each of these sentences. In some sentences, the verb has one word. In others, the verb has two words. On your paper, write the whole verb.

Sample Sentence The flagpole was shaking.

Verb was shaking.

1. I have seen *Star Wars* three times.
2. Carol is playing the trumpet.
3. Gary has done his homework.
4. The rabbit hopped behind the bush.
5. We have learned many new songs at camp.
6. The birds have eaten the cherries.
7. Anita paid the cashier.
8. The Yankees have won the World Series.

B. Number your paper from 1 to 8. Choose the correct verb in each sentence. Write the correct verb.

Sample Sentence Carlos (drawing, was drawing) a picture.

Correct Verb was drawing

1. Maria (eating, was eating) an orange.
2. Phil (reading, is reading) a new book.
3. I (have forgotten, forgotten) my sweater.
4. The janitor (waxing, is waxing) the floor.
5. The principal (has gone, gone) to a meeting.
6. Neil (is making, making) a salad.
7. Susan (watching, was watching) TV.
8. Sammy (done, has done) his best.

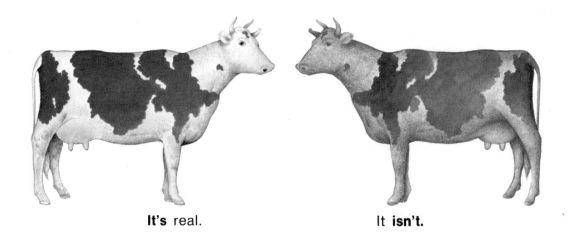

It's real.   It **isn't**.

Part 4 Using Contractions

A **contraction** is a word made by putting together
two other words. When the words are put together, at
least one letter is left out. An apostrophe is used in
place of the missing letter or letters.

Here are some examples of contractions.

I wi<u>ll</u> becomes <u>I</u>'ll
<u>she</u> i<u>s</u> becomes <u>she</u>'s
<u>she</u> ha<u>s</u> becomes <u>she</u>'s
<u>they</u> a<u>re</u> becomes <u>they</u>'re
<u>we</u> ha<u>ve</u> becomes <u>we</u>'ve
ha<u>s</u> <u>not</u> becomes ha<u>s</u>n't
<u>he</u> woul<u>d</u> becomes <u>he</u>'d

150

Notice how the underlined letters are used to form
the contraction. The letters that are not underlined
are not used in the contraction. An apostrophe is
used instead.

Some contractions are made by putting together a pronoun and a verb. Read this list of contractions. Notice where the apostrophes are used.

I am	I'm	we are	we're
I have	I've	we had	we'd
I will	I'll	we would	we'd
you are	you're	we will	we'll
he has	he's	you will	you'll
he is	he's	you have	you've
she will	she'll	they had	they'd
it is	it's	they will	they'll

Other contractions are made by putting together a verb and the word *not*. In a contraction, *not* always becomes *n't*.

is not	isn't	has not	hasn't
are not	aren't	have not	haven't
was not	wasn't	had not	hadn't
were not	weren't	can not	can't
should not	shouldn't	do not	don't
could not	couldn't	does not	doesn't
would not	wouldn't	did not	didn't

The words *will* and *not* form the contraction *won't*. This is the only contraction used often in which letters are dropped and other letters are changed.

151

won't

Exercises Using Contractions

A. Number your paper from 1 to 12. Make a contraction of each of the following pairs of words. Write the contraction on your paper.

Sample Words he is
Contraction he's

1. can not
2. you will
3. do not
4. I am

5. you are
6. could not
7. he is
8. will not

9. we are
10. they will
11. were not
12. we would

B. Copy the following contractions. After each contraction, write the two words it puts together.

Sample Contraction you've
Words you have

1. you've
2. aren't
3. wasn't
4. I've

5. shouldn't
6. haven't
7. won't
8. it's

9. she'll
10. weren't
11. hasn't
12. I'll

C. Copy the following contractions. Place the apostrophe where it belongs.

Sample Contraction theyll
Answer they'll

1. cant
2. wed
3. couldnt
4. wont

5. Im
6. shell
7. hes
8. youll

9. youre
10. were
11. havent
12. theyd

Part 5 Using Negatives Correctly

You have learned that some contractions are made by putting together a verb and the word *not*. Here are some examples.

$$was + not = wasn't$$
$$did + not = didn't$$
$$should + not = shouldn't$$

Words made in this way are called *not*-words.

There are some other words called *no*-words. Each of these words, except one, has *no* in it.

no	nobody	none	never
no one	nothing	nowhere	

The *not*-words and the *no*-words are called **negatives.** In a sentence, do not use a *not*-word and a *no*-word together.

Often it is best to leave out one of the negatives.

Wrong *Nobody didn't* come.
Right *Nobody* came.

Wrong I *don't* have *no* pencils.
Right I *don't* have *any* pencils.

Do not use a *not*-word and a *no*-word together.

Exercises   Using Negatives Correctly

A. Copy each of these sentences. Use the correct word.

> Sample Sentence Puzzles aren't (ever, never)
> easy.
> Answer Puzzles aren't ever easy.

1. The player didn't make (no, any) errors.
2. I haven't seen (any, no) bus go by.
3. Jennie has (ever, never) been to my house.
4. This book (has, hasn't) no pictures.
5. There aren't (no, any) letters for me.
6. The bare tree doesn't give (no, any) shade.
7. Anna won't smile at (anybody, nobody).
8. Roberto doesn't remember (nothing, anything) about his dream.
9. Our team hasn't scored (any, no) points.
10. I (haven't, have) never ridden an elephant.

B. Follow the directions for Exercise A.

1. Most spiders don't hurt (anybody, nobody).
2. I don't need (no, any) help.
3. Lee doesn't want (any, none) of the cake.
4. My dog doesn't bark at (nobody, anybody).
5. Charlie's team has never won (no, any) games.
6. I don't (ever, never) get sick.
7. My sister won't eat (any, no) onions.
8. John (has, hasn't) done nothing wrong.
9. The spaceman wasn't wearing (no, any) helmet.
10. The box didn't have (anything, nothing) in it.

More Exercises

Learning About Verbs

A. Finding Verbs (Use after page 140.)

Copy the following sentences. Underline the verb in each sentence.

1. Hens lay eggs.
2. The wind blew hard.
3. The tiger roared.
4. Mom sells houses.
5. Van petted the puppy.
6. The rabbit hopped away.
7. Travis does magic tricks.
8. My favorite show begins now.
9. Our class gave a play.
10. Birds fly south in the fall.

B. Using Two Kinds of Verbs. (Use after page 143.)

Copy each of the following sentences. Some have action verbs. Some have verbs that tell that something is. Underline the verbs.

1. The planets move around the sun.
2. I am sure about that answer.
3. The directions were clear.
4. An engineer drives the train.
5. The cashier gave me my ticket.
6. Danny forgot his book.

7. You are very thoughtful.
8. The hawk flew high.
9. My vacation was fun.
10. Shelley wore her raincoat.

C. Using Helping Verbs   (Use after page 148.)

Number your paper from 1 to 10. Find the verb in each of these sentences. In some sentences, the verb has one word. In others, the verb has two words. On your paper, write the whole verb.

1. Bill has been a Cub Scout for one year.
2. Carter and Janet have gone to a movie.
3. The driver honked his horn.
4. The arrow points north.
5. Marla is jumping rope.
6. Spencer was writing a letter.
7. The wind blew the paper away.
8. The skier has broken his leg.
9. Tanya crawled into the cave.
10. Misako is bouncing the ball.

D. Using Contractions   (Use after page 151.)

Copy the following contractions. Place the apostrophe where it belongs.

1. doesnt	5. wouldnt	9. hasnt
2. dont	6. werent	10. theyre
3. well	7. didnt	11. Ive
4. hadnt	8. Ill	12. arent

E. Using Negatives Correctly   (Use after page 153.)

Copy each of these sentences. Use the correct word.

1. Don't tell (no one, anyone) this secret.
2. I didn't forget (nothing, anything).
3. David didn't go (anywhere, nowhere).
4. My cat won't (ever, never) come to me.
5. The store doesn't sell (any, no) bread.
6. I don't want (any, none) of that candy.
7. Jean (has, hasn't) never seen any deer.
8. I have never won (nothing, anything).
9. My sister won't play (any, no) games.
10. You shouldn't tell (any, no) lies.

Chapter 12

Using Verbs Correctly

Look at the picture on the opposite page. Try to tell what is happening in the picture.

The words you used to tell what is happening are verbs. A verb tells about an action or tells that something is.

However, this is not all a verb does. The form of a verb can change. Some forms show that the action is happening now. Other forms show that the action has already happened. This chapter will help you use the different forms of verbs correctly.

Part 1 Verbs That Tell About Present Time

Some verbs tell about things that are happening right now. Here are some examples.

Ted *is* at a parade. He *listens* to a band.
Jill *has* a hobby. She *collects* model cars.

We say that verbs like this are in the **present time.**

Verbs in the present time have two forms. One form is the basic form. Examples are *ride, play,* and *see.*

The other form is the basic form with an *s* added. This is called the *-s* form. Examples are *rides, plays,* and *sees.* There is only one correct verb form for each sentence. The correct verb form depends on the subject of the sentence.

Read these sample sentences. They show the correct way to use the basic form and the *-s* form of verbs.

Keith *rides* his bike.
The boys *ride* their bikes.
Libby *plays* baseball.
The girls *play* baseball.
The rabbit *sees* the garden.
The rabbits *see* the garden.

Every verb used with a singular subject has the *-s* form. Every verb used with a plural subject has the basic form.

Verbs used with the pronouns *I* and *you* do not follow the rule. The word *I* stands for one person. However, it is always used with the basic form of the verb. The word *you* may stand for one or more than one person. It, too, is always used with the basic form of a verb.

I *ride* my bike.   You *ride* your bike.

Use the basic form of a verb with a plural subject.

Use the *-s* form of a verb with a singular subject.

Usually it is not hard to change the basic form of a verb to the *-s* form. Sometimes, however, you must make some spelling changes. Follow these rules.

1. If the basic verb form ends in *s, x, ch,* or *sh,* add -es to make the -s form.

    s The players *pass* the ball.
        Juan *passes* the ball.
    x The workers *fix* radios.
        Carla *fixes* radios.
  ch The butterflies *touch* the flowers.
        The butterfly *touches* the flowers.
  sh The shoppers *push* the carts.
        Each shopper *pushes* a cart.

2. Some verbs have a basic form that ends in *y* following a consonant. Change the *y* to *i* and add -es.

carry   The horses *carry* riders.
        My horse *carries* me.

Exercises Using Verbs That Tell About Present Time

A. Number your paper from 1 to 8. Read each of the following sentences. Find the subject and the verb. Write the subject. Write whether the subject is *singular* or *plural*. Then write the verb.

> Sample Question The players need a rest.
> Answer players, plural, need

1. Molly carries the heavy book easily.
2. The people hear the church bells on Sunday.
3. Leaves change color in the fall.
4. My cat chases birds.
5. Airplanes fly over my house.
6. Athletes practice every day.
7. That door closes too quickly.
8. This key opens the door.

B. Number your paper from 1 to 8. Choose the correct form of the verb. Write it down.

> Sample Question Julia (keep, keeps) a diary.
> Answer keeps

1. Ghosts (howl, howls) in the haunted house.
2. This paint (dry, dries) fast.
3. My shoelace (trip, trips) me.
4. The mother duck (leads, lead) the ducklings.
5. Elephants (travel, travels) in herds.
6. Flowers (grow, grows) best in sunlight.
7. Our dog (bury, buries) his bones in the yard.
8. The green cup (leak, leaks).

Part 2 Verbs That Tell About Past Time

Some verbs tell about action that has already happened. The action is finished. Here are some examples.

Ted *was* at a parade. He *listened* to a band.
Jill *had* a hobby. She *collected* model cars.

We say that verbs like this are in the **past time.**

There are three different ways that verbs can tell about past actions.

1. The first way is to change the ending of the basic form.

    talk   talked

2. The second way is to use helping verbs.

    talk   have talked

3. Certain verbs use a third way. They change the basic form itself.

    write   wrote

You will now learn more about these three ways.

163

Changing the Ending of the Basic Form

You can make most verbs tell about the past by adding -ed to the basic form.

cook   cooked

stay   stayed

laugh   laughed

Sometimes, you must make spelling changes. Follow these rules when you write verbs in the past time.

1. When the basic form ends in silent *e*, drop the final *e*. Then add -ed.

rak<u>e</u>   rak<u>ed</u>

plac<u>e</u>   plac<u>ed</u>

mov<u>e</u>   mov<u>ed</u>

2. When the basic form ends in *y* after a consonant, change the *y* to *i*. Then add -ed.

hurr<u>y</u>   hurr<u>ied</u>

worr<u>y</u>   worr<u>ied</u>

cop<u>y</u>   cop<u>ied</u>

3. When the basic form ends in a single consonant after a single short vowel, double the final consonant. Then add -ed.

sto<u>p</u>   sto<u>pped</u>

fi<u>b</u>   fi<u>bbed</u>

pa<u>t</u>   pa<u>tted</u>

Using Helping Verbs

The second way to make verbs show the past is to use helping verbs. You use *has* or *have* or *had* with the *-ed* form of the verb.

Vincent *studied* the violin.
He *has studied* for a year.
Faith and Eddie *worked* on a project.
They *have worked* together before.
Donna *laughed* at the clown.
She *had laughed* at all his tricks.

Use *has* with a singular subject. Use *have* with a plural subject. Use *had* with either a singular or a plural subject.

Changing the Basic Form

There are some verbs that change their basic form to show past time.

come   came
lose   lost
find   found

Some of these verbs change their basic form again to show past time with a helping verb.

come   came   has come
see   saw   has seen
do   did   has done

Many of these verbs are used often. You should know which verbs change their forms. You should know which forms tell about the past by themselves. You should know which forms go with helping verbs.

Below is a chart of ten verbs you use often. These verbs change to show past time. Study the chart. Look at the chart when you are not sure which form to use in your writing.

Verbs That Change To Show the Past

Present	Past Alone	Past with Helping Verbs
break	broke	broken
bring	brought	brought
come	came	come
do	did	done
eat	ate	eaten
give	gave	given
go	went	gone
run	ran	run
see	saw	seen
take	took	taken

The puppy **eats** quickly.   The puppy **has eaten.**

Exercises   Using Verbs That Tell About Past Time

A. Copy each of these verbs. Then add *-ed* to each verb to show past time. Make any spelling change that is needed.

Sample Question bake
          Answer bake, baked

1. walk	5. taste	9. push
2. play	6. use	10. try
3. hop	7. show	11. train
4. cry	8. rip	12. carry

B. Copy each of these verbs. Then add *-ed* and a helping verb to show past time. Make any spelling change needed.

Sample Question hurry
          Answer hurry, has hurried

1. touch	5. remember	9. look
2. pin	6. stop	10. scratch
3. want	7. dance	11. worry
4. study	8. smile	12. invite

C. Number your paper from 1 to 10. In some of these sentences the verb should tell about present time. In other sentences, it should tell about past time. Choose the correct verb form. Write the correct form on your paper.

> Sample Question 1 Yesterday Joel (hears, heard) a new song.
>
> Answer 1 heard
>
> Sample Question 2 My dog always (hears, heard) me when I call him.
>
> Answer 2 hears

1. Jamie (stays, stayed) home last week with a cold.
2. Tulips (grow, grew) in our garden each spring.
3. We (take, took) a hike yesterday.
4. Mom always (leaves, left) for work at eight o'clock.
5. Billy (rides, rode) his bike every day.
6. On her last birthday Leah (is, was) eight years old.
7. I (eat, ate) hamburgers for supper last night.
8. Doctors (help, helped) people when they are sick.
9. Meg (sees, saw) the frog before it hopped away.
10. The farmer (plants, planted) the beans last spring.

More Exercises

Using Verbs Correctly

A. Using Verbs That Tell About the Present Time
(Use after page 161.)

Number your paper from 1 to 10. Choose the correct form of the verb. Write it down.

1. Steve (likes, like) bananas.
2. Shadows (grow, grows) long in the afternoon.
3. Sean (collect, collects) coins.
4. Mr. Maxwell (fix, fixes) clocks.
5. Children (love, loves) parades.
6. Dogs (barks, bark) at strangers.
7. Mary (dislike, dislikes) red jelly beans.
8. Ants always (comes, come) to our picnics.
9. These shoes (costs, cost) too much.
10. The elevator (stops, stop) on the first floor.

B. Using Verbs That Tell About Past Time
(Use after page 166.)

Copy each of these verbs. Then add -ed and a helping verb to show past time. Make any spelling change that is needed.

1. tap   5. mop   9. bake
2. hike   6. love   10. bury
3. fry   7. paint   11. toss
4. call   8. ask   12. bat

Chapter 13

Writing
a Story

There are many ways to tell a story.

You can act it out.
You can sing it.
You can draw pictures.
You can say it out loud.
You can write it in paragraphs.

Every story is different. Yet all stories are alike in some ways. In every story something happens. It happens to someone. It happens somewhere.

In this chapter you will learn about stories. You will study one-paragraph stories. You will study longer ones, too. You will also write stories of your own.

Part 1 The Characters

A story tells about someone. The someone is called a character.

Writing About Real Characters

Some stories have one character. Others have more than one. Sometimes the writer of a story is a character in the story. Read the following story. The writer tells about something that happened to her.

Last Saturday I washed my favorite jeans. I put them into the machine. I poured in a whole box of soap. Then I went upstairs. An hour later I opened the basement door. Soapsuds were everywhere! It took two days for them to disappear.

The writer uses the word *I*. This shows that she is writing about herself. How many *I*'s can you find in the story?

A character can also be someone the writer knows. It might be the old woman next door, or a friend's big brother, or a classmate.

Here is a story. It tells about the writer's cousin.

My cousin Rosa has a big maple tree in her yard. Last fall she raked the leaves into piles. She jumped and rolled in them. She built a playhouse with many leaf-rooms. Then she packed her leaf-house into a bag. She carried it to the alley.

Read this story. Then tell whether the character is the writer, or someone the writer knows.

My bike picked up speed. Down the hill, faster and faster I went. I squeezed the hand brakes. Nothing happened. I couldn't slow down. I couldn't stop. At that moment I saw three garbage cans. I steered toward them. Bang, clang, into the cans I crashed. The bike flew one way. I flew another. We both landed safely.

Writing About Made-Up Characters

A character can be made up by the writer. Kermit the Frog and Mighty Mouse were made up by writers. Snoopy and the Pied Piper were made up by the writers. Can you name other made-up characters?

Exercise Telling About a Made-Up Character

Read this story. Then answer the question.

Tillie Troll could not sleep. Her fur was scratchy. She had eaten three desserts. Now her stomach hurt. Tillie tossed and turned. She stared at the ceiling of her cave. Bats were hanging there asleep. She began to count them. One bat. Two bats. Three bats. Soon she was fast asleep too.

173

Who is the made-up character?

Part 2 The Setting

A story happens somewhere. It might happen in any of these places.

high in the trees   in a closet
on the moon   in a basement
underground   in an empty house
                    on a cloud
                    in a cave

Where a story happens is called the **setting**.

Exercise Telling About the Setting

Read this story. Then answer the questions.

Owl was at home. He was eating buttered toast and hot pea soup for supper. Owl heard a loud sound at the front door. He opened his door wide. Winter came into the house. It came in fast. A cold wind pushed Owl against the wall. It blew out the fire in the fireplace. It made the window shades flap and shiver. It turned the pea soup into hard, green ice. The wind blew around and around. Then Winter rushed out and slammed the front door. —ARNOLD LOBEL

174

What is the setting?
Can you draw a picture of this setting?

Part 3   What Happens?

A story tells about something that happened. Read this story. Think about what happens.

Inside the cramped and crowded egg, a robin was curled up tightly. It had been growing in the egg for nearly two weeks. Now it was ready to hatch. It began to peck at the eggshell. It pecked until it had chipped a small hole in the shell. Peeping softly, it poked its beak out into the world. After that it fell asleep.   —RUSSELL FREEDMAN

The story is about a robin. It is the *character*. The robin is inside an egg. That is the *setting*.

What happens in the story?

1. The robin is curled up tightly.
2. It is ready to hatch.
3. It pecks at the eggshell.
4. It chips a hole in the shell.
5. It pokes its beak out.
6. It falls asleep.

Exercises Telling What Happens

A. Look at this comic strip. Then answer these questions.

1. Who is the character?
2. What is the setting?

B. Write one sentence for each box. Tell what happens.

C. Here is the first sentence of a story about Homer. Finish the paragraph. Use your sentences from Exercise B.

Homer had a loose tooth.

D. Check your story.

1. Is the first line indented?
2. Does Homer's name begin with a capital letter?
3. Does each sentence begin with a capital letter?
4. Does each sentence end with a period?

Part 4 Writing One-Paragraph Stories

When you write a story, first think about it. Ask yourself these questions.

1. Who will be the character?

A monster with big teeth?
Your best friend?
Yourself?

2. What will be the setting?

Your neighborhood?
A faraway place?
A make-believe land?

3. What will happen?

An exciting adventure?
Something sad?
Something frightening?

Next, write the first sentence of your story. Name the character. Try to name the setting, too.

Then write the rest of the sentences. Tell what happens to the character.

Finally, check your story.

1. Is the first line indented?
2. Does the character's name begin with a capital letter?
3. Does each sentence begin with a capital letter?
4. Does each sentence end with a period?

Exercise   Writing a Story

Choose one of these story ideas. Copy the first sentence. Then write five or six sentences telling what happened. Check your finished story.

1. Anita lives in a big city. She is riding the bus downtown. Tell about her trip.

First sentence Anita got on the bus and sat next to a window.

2. Think about your dreams. Were any of them exciting? Were any frightening? Choose one dream. Tell about it.

First sentence Once I dreamed that I _____.

3. Wiggly Worm wants to know more about people. He visits someone's kitchen. Tell what happens to him.

First sentence Wiggly Worm crawled under the screen door.

Part 5 Writing Longer Stories

Some stories are one paragraph. Others are longer. Here is a story with three paragraphs. As you read, keep these questions in mind.

1. Who are the characters?
2. What is the setting?
3. What happens?

Country Mouse Learns a Lesson

Country Mouse was poor. He had only stale bread and dry cheese to eat. His cousin City Mouse lived in a beautiful house. He nibbled the finest cheese. He ate cake with frosting every day.

City Mouse invited Country Mouse to visit his fine house. Country Mouse agreed. Late at night he arrived at his cousin's door. City Mouse led him to the kitchen. There they began to feast on leftovers from a big party. Suddenly the mice heard barking. A huge dog rushed into the room. They barely escaped with their lives.

That same night Country Mouse went home. He had learned a lesson. He had learned that plain food, eaten in peace, tastes better than fine food, eaten without peace.

Who are the characters? City Mouse and Country Mouse

What is the setting? City Mouse's House

What happens?

1. City Mouse invites Country Mouse to visit.
2. Country Mouse agrees.
3. Country Mouse goes to City Mouse's house.
4. The mice go to the kitchen.
5. They begin to eat leftovers.
6. They hear barking.
7. A dog rushes into the room.
8. The mice run.
9. Country Mouse goes home.

The Title of a Story

Often a longer story has a **title.** It is written above the story. It tells what the story is about.

The first word of a title begins with a capital letter. So do the other important words.

The story about City Mouse and Country Mouse has a title. The title is "Country Mouse Learns a Lesson." Which words begin with capital letters?

Writing and Checking Your Story

When you write your story on your paper, you should be thinking of what happens in the story.

When you are done, check what you have written.

Guides for Checking Your Story

1. Is each paragraph indented?
2. Do the names of the characters begin with capital letters?
3. Does each sentence begin with a capital letter?
4. Does each sentence end with a period?
5. Does the story have a title?
6. Does the first word in the title begin with a capital letter?
7. Do other important words in the title begin with capital letters?

Exercises   Writing a Longer Story

A. Here are two story beginnings. Choose one. Then write at least two more paragraphs. Tell what happens to the character. Write a title for the story.

1. I stood on the porch in my Halloween costume. The moon was full. Wind sighed through the bare trees. I pressed the bell once, twice. The dark house was silent. Suddenly the door flew open.

2. I, Nate the Great, was drying off from the rain. I was sitting under a blanket and reading a detective book. My dog Sludge was sniffing it. I was on page 33 when I heard a knock. I opened the door.

—MARJORIE WEINMAN SHARMAT

B. Now check your story. Use the guides above. Make a final copy of your story.

Chapter 14

Making Clear Explanations

You have studied paragraphs. This is what you have learned.

1. A paragraph is a group of sentences.
2. A paragraph explains one idea.

This is what you have learned to do.

1. Give a main idea in a topic sentence.
2. Tell more about the main idea.

In this chapter you will study two kinds of paragraphs. You will learn about paragraphs that explain *how*. You will learn about paragraphs that explain *why*.

Part 1 Explaining *How*

Some paragraphs tell how to do something. Others tell how to make something. Both are called *how* paragraphs.

Here is a *how* paragraph. What is it about?

You can make butter from cream. Pour about half a pint of heavy cream into a big bowl. Beat it. First it will turn into whipped cream. Keep on beating. It will change. Part of it will become watery, and part will be little pale yellow lumps. Pour out the water. Spread the rest on bread.

—ALIKI

The paragraph tells how to do something. It tells how to make butter.

Exercise Studying *How* Paragraphs

Read each *how* paragraph. Complete the sentence after it.

Paragraph 1

Making popcorn is easy. First, pour oil into a pan. Next, sprinkle popcorn into the oil. Then put the lid on the pan and turn on the stove. Use low heat. Soon the popcorn will start to pop. When it stops popping, remove the pan from the heat. Turn off the heat. Take off the cover.

The paragraph tells how to _____.

Paragraph 2

Here's how to cross the street safely. Stand on the curb. Look to the right. Look to the left. Be sure that no cars are turning the corner. Then cross.

The paragraph tells how to _____.

The Topic Sentence

The first sentence in a *how* paragraph is usually the topic sentence. It tells what the paragraph is about. Study these two topic sentences.

1. Peeling a banana is as easy as one, two, three.
2. Would you like to make paste?

The first paragraph will tell how to peel a banana. The second paragraph will tell how to make paste.

Exercises   Studying Topic Sentences

A. Read the three topic sentences. Explain what each paragraph will be about.

1. Turning a cartwheel is fun.
2. Here's how to clean a gerbil's cage.
3. Riding a two-wheel bike is easy.

B. List five things that you can do. Choose one to write about. Then complete *one* of these sentences.

185

It's easy to _____.
It's fun to _____.
Here's how to _____.

Writing a *How* Paragraph

The topic sentence of a *how* paragraph tells *what* to do or *what* to make. The rest of the sentences tell *how* to do it or *how* to make it. Read this paragraph.

You can make a musical instrument out of things from the kitchen. First, find two foil pie pans, a handful of dried beans, and a roll of tape. Next, put the beans into one of the plates. Put the other plate upside down over it. Then tape the edges of the plates together.

What is the paragraph about? It is about making a musical instrument.
How do you make a musical instrument?

1. First, you find pans, beans, and tape.
2. Next, you put the beans into one plate.
3. You put the other plate over it.
4. Then you tape the plates together.

The directions tell exactly what to do. They are in order. They tell what to do first, what to do second, what to do third, and what to do fourth. The words *first, next,* and *then* help to make the order clear.

Exercises Writing *How* Paragraphs

A. Below are two groups of sentences. The first explains how to make a shake. The second tells how to play a game. The sentences in each group are out of order. Read them.

1. a. Then turn on the blender for ten seconds.
   b. Here's how to make a great shake.
   c. Next, add one tablespoon of honey and one banana.
   d. After mixing, pour the shake into a tall glass.
   e. First, put one cup of milk and one-half cup of yogurt into a blender.
2. a. Next, line up behind the leader.
   b. When a player makes a mistake, that player becomes the new leader.
   c. You and your friends can play Follow the Leader.
   d. Then do whatever the leader does.
   e. First, choose a leader.

Now do this for each group of sentences.

1. Pick out the topic sentence.
2. Write it on a sheet of paper.
3. Find the words *first, next,* and *then.*
4. Write the steps in order.
5. Write the sentences as a paragraph. Be sure to indent the first line.

B. Take out the topic sentence you wrote earlier in this lesson. List the directions that you want to give. Add words that show order. Then write your paragraph.

Part 2 Explaining *Why*

How paragraphs tell how to do or make something. In Part 1 you studied *how* paragraphs. In Part 2 you will study another kind of paragraph. You will learn about *why* paragraphs.

Giving Reasons

How would you answer these questions?

1. What is the best program on television?
2. Who is the nicest person on your street?
3. Do dogs or cats make better pets?

You might give answers like these.

1. "Little House on the Prairie" is the best program on television.
2. Old Mr. Kelly is the nicest person on my street.
3. Cats make better pets than dogs.

You might also give reasons for each answer. Here is an example.

Cats make better pets than dogs.
Cats are cleaner.
Cats are quieter.   — Reasons
Cats are more independent.

The reasons explain why you think cats make better pets.

Exercise   Writing Reasons

Answer each question. Use a complete sentence.

1. Would you like to live on the moon?
2. Would a dragon make a good pet?
3. What is the best season of the year?
4. What is the most delicious sandwich?
5. Who is the nicest person you know?

Choose one of your answers. List three reasons for that answer. Write each reason as a complete sentence.

Giving Reasons in a Paragraph

You can give reasons in a paragraph. This kind of paragraph is a *why* paragraph.

The first sentence in a *why* paragraph is usually the topic sentence. It tells what you think. The rest of the sentences tell why.

Here is a *why* paragraph.

I like school. I am in a room with my friends. Every Friday the whole class goes to the library. Once a month we go on a field trip.

The writer tells what she thinks in the first sentence. She says that she likes school. Then she explains why. She gives three reasons.

1. I am in a room with my friends.
2. Every Friday the whole class goes to the library.
3. Once a month we go on a field trip.

The writer uses complete sentences. She indents the first line.

Exercise Giving Reasons in a Paragraph

Choose one of these topics.

food	weather
sports	games
clothes	vacations

Think about things you like about the topic. Think about things you don't like about it. Then complete one of these sentences.

I like _____.
I don't like _____.

List three reasons why. Use complete sentences. Finally, write your four sentences as a paragraph.

Writing Paragraphs

The topic sentence tells *what* you want to do. The rest of the sentences tell *why* you want to do it.
Read this paragraph.

    I want to go to Grandma's house on my birthday. I can play her piano. She will bake a big birthday cake. She will let me stay up late.

What does the writer want to do? What reasons does he give?
The writer explains *why* in a paragraph. He uses complete sentences. He indents the first line.

Exercise   Writing a Paragraph

Complete this sentence.

I want to _____. **191**

List three reasons why. Write complete sentences. Finally, write the four sentences as a paragraph.

Chapter 15

Learning About Adjectives

Part 1 What Are Adjectives?

Look at the picture on page 192. Name some of the things you see in the picture.

The words you use to name those things are nouns.

Now let's choose one thing in the picture. Let's talk about the horse.

The word *horse* tells the name of the thing. It does not tell any more about the thing. To tell more, you need more words.

Read these sentences. Choose the one that tells more about the horse in the picture.

> The girl rode a sleepy old horse.
> The girl rode a graceful black horse.
> The girl rode a shiny yellow horse.

The only words that changed in these sentences were *adjectives*. **Adjectives** are words that *describe* nouns. That means they tell more about the nouns.

The first sample sentence was this.

> The girl rode a sleepy old horse.

The adjectives are *sleepy* and *old*. They make you think of one kind of horse.

The second sample sentence was this.

> The girl rode a graceful black horse.

The adjectives are *graceful* and *black*. They make you think of a different kind of horse.

This was the third sample sentence.

> The girl rode a shiny yellow horse.

Can you find the adjectives in this sentence? This is the only sentence that tells about the picture. The adjectives *shiny* and *yellow* describe the horse in the picture. The adjectives that are different make you think of horses that are different.

You can use an adjective before the noun it describes.

The bear had brown fur.

Brown describes *fur*.

You can also use an adjective after the noun it describes.

Its fur is brown.

Brown still describes *fur*.

There are several kinds of adjectives.

Adjectives That Tell What Kind

Many adjectives tell what kind of thing the noun is. Here are some adjectives of this kind. These adjectives were in the sample sentences.

shiny   graceful   old   black
brown   yellow   sleepy

Notice that *shiny* and *sleepy* both end in *-y*. Many adjectives that tell what kind end in *-y*.

Adjectives That Tell How Many

Number words are adjectives that tell how many.

one   two   twenty   fifty

Other adjectives that tell how many do not tell exact numbers.

some   many   more   several

Adjectives That Tell Which Ones

Some adjectives point out nouns. They are adjectives that tell which ones. The most important adjectives in this group are *this, that, these,* and *those.*

Use *this* and *that* with singular nouns.

this bird   that bird

This tells about something close. *That* tells about something farther away.

Use *these* and *those* with plural nouns.

these birds   those birds

These tells about close things. *Those* tells about faraway things.

196

Never use *them* as an adjective. It is a pronoun. It stands for a noun. It does not point out a noun.

Exercises Using Adjectives

A. Copy each of these sentences. Draw a circle around every noun. Draw a line under every adjective. Be able to tell which noun the adjective describes.

Sample Question 1 The frog is green.
Answer 1 The (frog) is green.

Sample Question 2 Kermit is a green frog.
Answer 2 (Kermit) is a green (frog.)

1. The kitten chased the red ball.
2. That family has five people.
3. Dale went to a funny movie.
4. The sky is blue.
5. The cow ate some clover.
6. This hot cocoa is good.
7. Farmers plant many crops.
8. Fresh cider is delicious.
9. The friendly policeman gave directions.
10. The janitor oiled the squeaky door.

B. Number your paper from 1 to 10. Choose the correct adjective for each sentence. Write the correct adjective.

Sample Question Sit on (this, that) chair here.
Answer this

1. (This, That) famous bridge is far from here.
2. (Them, Those) students won the prize.
3. (These, Them) boxes are heavy.
4. (Them, Those) papers fell from the board.
5. Please leave (those, these) chairs over there.

197

6. (Those, These) girls with me are on the team.
7. The bus stops at (this, that) sign over there.
8. (Those, Them) trees are maple trees.
9. I painted (those, them) pictures.
10. (Them, Those) toys are broken.

C. Add an adjective of any kind to each of these nouns. Write the adjective and noun.

Sample Question shoes
Possible Answer two shoes

1. puppy	4. carrots	7. story
2. hamburger	5. game	8. giant
3. bed	6. tree	9. hair

D. Add an adjective of any kind to each of these sentences. Write your new sentence.

Sample Question The children played a game.
Possible Answer The five children played a game.
The children played a noisy game.

1. Clouds float through the sky.
2. The girl clapped her hands.
3. Mother planted flowers.
4. My jacket is in the closet.
5. The boy gathered branches.
6. Joanna found shells at the beach.
7. Our club has a password.
8. The mouse ran away.

Part 2   Using *A*, *An*, and *The*

The words *a, an,* and *the* are adjectives. They are a special kind of adjective. Follow these rules when you use them.

1. **You may use *the* before singular nouns or plural nouns.**

    the monster   *the* monsters

2. **You may use *a* or *an* before singular nouns only.**

    a friend   *an* enemy

3. **Use *a* before words beginning with consonant sounds.**

    a hawk   *a* brown owl

4. **Use *an* before words beginning with vowel sounds.**

    an owl
    an angry hawk

Exercises   Using *A*, *An*, and *The*

A. Copy each of the following sentences. Fill in the blank with *a* or *an*. Remember to think of the sound that begins the word after the blank.

> Sample Question I heard _____ noise.
> Answer I heard a noise.

1. _____ insect has six legs.
2. I need _____ empty box.
3. Tina read _____ magazine.
4. May I have _____ orange?
5. Kara saw _____ ostrich at the zoo.
6. The band played _____ march.
7. Do you want _____ egg for breakfast?
8. The Scouts camped near _____ river.
9. _____ ant crawled across the floor.
10. Sean ordered _____ bowl of soup.

B. Follow the directions for Exercise A.

1. Harold bought _____ ice cream cone.
2. Did you ride _____ sled?
3. _____ elephant likes peanuts.
4. Mr. Warren is _____ plumber.
5. _____ icicle fell on me.
6. The cook wore _____ apron.
7. The hikers rested on _____ bench.
8. This tree looks like _____ oak.
9. Would you read _____ story to me?
10. _____ canoe moves very quietly.

More Exercises

Learning About Adjectives

A. Using Adjectives (Use after page 196.)

Copy each of these sentences. Draw a circle around every noun. Draw a line under every adjective.

1. Loud noises scare young children.
2. Lucky Matthew found some quarters.
3. Many ships carry bulky loads.
4. These shoes are comfortable.
5. This huge library holds many books.
6. One old man sat on that orange bench.
7. Playful monkeys swung in large cages.
8. That sly fox caught several chickens.
9. Roberto likes crunchy peanuts.
10. Those green plants are healthy.

B. Using *A, An,* and *The* (Use after page 199.)

Copy each sentence. Fill in the blank with *a* or *an.*

1. The robin built _____ nest.
2. I ran from _____ angry bee.
3. Luke watched _____ soccer game on TV.
4. Heather climbed _____ apple tree.
5. _____ alligator has a long nose.
6. We live in _____ old house.
7. The cat sleeps on _____ pillow.
8. Darrell has _____ black eye.

Chapter 16

Telling Stories

Do you like to tell stories? People love to listen
to a good storyteller. They can picture the story.
It seems real to them.

To make a story interesting, you must plan it
carefully. You don't want to forget anything.

Use your voice to make your story sound lively. Let
your whole body help you tell the story.

Now let's see how a good story is put together.

Part 1 Discovering the Parts of a Story

A story has three parts. They are the beginning, the middle, and the end.

The beginning paragraph gets the story started. The first sentences answer many of these **w** questions.

w Questions

Who?

What?

Where?

When?

Why?

The middle of the story builds suspense. Each sentence tells something that happens. The most important sentence gives the *climax*. The **climax** is the peak of the story, the most exciting moment.

After the climax comes the end of the story. It tells how everything works out. The last sentences tie the whole story together.

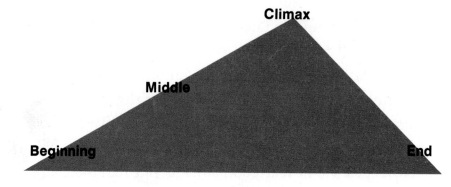

Now let's read a story that Marsha tells to her class.

A Mountain Scare

Last summer we went to the Rocky Mountains for a vacation. There were five of us—Mom, Dad, Hank, Patty, and I.

Early one morning we decided to drive high up into the mountains. We stopped many times to look at the view. Sometimes we got out of the car. One time I was helping my parents get our picnic lunch ready. My little brother and sister walked over to a rock to play. Suddenly my mom looked up. She couldn't see Hank and Patty anywhere! Mom was scared. She thought they had fallen over the side of the mountain. She screamed and ran toward the rock.

Just then, Patty and Hank stuck their heads up over the rock. They had been safe all along. My mom was upset, though. She and my dad kept us close to them during the rest of the trip.

Exercise Discovering the Parts of a Story

Think about Marsha's story. Answer these questions. You will need to read parts of the story again.

1. Which **w** questions does Marsha answer in the beginning of the story?

2. Next Marsha tells the middle of the story. Read it again. Marsha tells what happened, step by step. What is the climax of the story? Write the climax sentence.

Marsha ends her story with these sentences.

Just then, Patty and Hank stuck their heads up over the rock. They had been safe all along. My mom was upset, though. She and my dad kept us close to them during the rest of the trip.

The end of the story ties the events together. Read these questions and answer them in class.

1. Where were Hank and Patty? Read the sentence aloud that gives you the answer.

2. How did Marsha's mom feel? Read the word that describes her feelings.

3. The scare made Marsha's parents change. What did they do during the rest of the trip?

Part 2 Telling a Story About Yourself

Now you are ready to tell a story about something that happened to you.

First, think about what to tell. What is the most exciting thing you have ever done? Perhaps that will make a good story.

Now plan the beginning of your story. It should be two or three sentences long. In the beginning, tell the answers to some of the **W** questions.

Next plan the middle of your story. The last sentence in the middle paragraph should be the climax sentence.

Here are some examples of climax sentences.

1. At last my dog opened his eyes, and we knew he would be all right.
2. The tornado roared over us as we slammed the basement door.
3. When I walked into the room, everyone began singing "Happy Birthday."
4. My dad opened the back door and shouted, "You have a new baby sister!"
5. Just as I was about to give up, I felt a strong pull on my fishing line.

The end of your story comes after the climax. Be sure to tie everything together in your last sentences.

Telling Your Story Out Loud

Decide how to end your story. Your last sentence should bring the story to a close. It should be strong enough to let your audience know you are finished.

You do not need to memorize your story. Instead, learn the events in order. Then tell your story. When you finish, pause and then return to your seat.

Guides for Telling a Story About Yourself

1. Stand or sit straight.
2. Look at your listeners.
3. Keep your mind on the events in your story.
4. Speak clearly and loudly enough to be heard.
5. End your story with a strong sentence.

Exercises   Telling a Story About Yourself

A. These sentences are the last sentences in four different stories. Talk about the sentences in class. Which ones are strong? Which ones are not strong?

1. We landed safely, and I guess that's all I have to say. I mean, that's the whole story.
2. My dad called the police. After our scare, we never let strangers into our house again.
3. And the kittens looked like little furry balls, and there isn't any more to tell, so I'll sit down now.
4. We shoveled snow all day. That night we drank hot cocoa and fell sound asleep. Our family was safe.

B. Here is a list of events in a story that Tony told to his class. The first and last sentences are in the right place. Some of the other sentences are in the wrong order. They are marked with a star.

Tony's Story

1. My parents gave me a new bike for my birthday.

*2. There were ten people in the race.

3. I decided to enter the Glendale Bike Race.

4. I tried hard, but I couldn't get into the front ranks.

5. I began to think I could never win.

*6. I had won the bike race!

7. Then, all of a sudden, the lead rider slowed down.

8. I pedaled harder than I ever had before.

*9. With a last effort, I raced across the finish line.

10. I moved into third place, then second, then first.

11. Later, I received a beautiful trophy.

12. It was the happiest day in my life.

Copy the events on your paper. Place them in the right order. Then draw a line under the climax sentence.

C. Write out a story about something that happened to you. Learn the events in your story. Then practice telling your story to a friend.

D. Tell your story to the class. Follow the Guides for Telling a Story About Yourself.

Part 3 Telling a Class Story

You and your class will tell a story together. It will be about a monster who comes to your school. The story must have a beginning, a middle, and an end. Your teacher will write the story on the board.

First, you should talk together about the story. Decide on the answers to the **W** questions. Second, name the events that will fill the middle of the story. Make up a climax sentence. Then talk about the end of the story.

When you tell a class story, you must share ideas. Everyone may add something to the story, but not every idea can be used. You must work together to tell a story that makes sense.

Guides for Telling a Class Story

1. Talk together about the beginning, middle, and end.
2. Let everyone make up a sentence to go into the story.
3. Arrange the sentences in an order that makes sense.
4. Combine ideas. Take out sentences or ideas that don't fit.
5. Reread the whole story together.

Exercises   Telling a Class Story

A. Talk together about your monster story. Decide on the answers to these questions. Use strong adjectives and verbs.

1. Who is the monster?
2. What is the monster doing?
3. Where is the monster?
4. When did the monster arrive?
5. Why is the monster at your school?

B. Choose the events that will go into the middle of your story. Begin by answering these questions.

1. What adventure do you have with the monster?
2. What is the most exciting thing that happens with the monster?

C. Write out the climax sentence of your story.

D. Talk about the end of the story. How will you tie everything together?

E. Now finish your class story. Follow the Guides for Telling a Class Story. You may want to draw pictures to go with the story. Some people might like to act it out for the rest of the class.

Chapter 17

Writing a Description

Picture a dog in your mind.

Is the dog big or small? Thin or fat?
What color is its hair? Is it long or short?
Are the dog's ears pointed or floppy?
Does the dog have a long or a short tail?

When you answer these questions, you are telling how the dog looks. You are **describing** the dog.

In this chapter, you will learn ways to describe people and things. You will learn to use words that describe. You will learn to write sentences that describe. You will develop paragraphs that describe.

213

Part 1   Words That Describe

There are many kinds of words that describe. You need to study a person or thing closely. Then you can decide which words are best to use. Do you want to describe size? shape? color?

Words That Describe Size

Some words describe size. Here are some size words.

huge   large
tiny   long
big   short
little enormous
small   tall

What other size words do you know?

Size words tell how big someone or something looks.

tall trees
a huge glass of milk
a small cupcake

What word describes the size of an elephant? What word describes the size of a ladybug?

Words That Describe Shape

Some words describe shape. Here are a few shape words.

round   curved
flat   pointed
square   hilly
thin   winding
fat   crooked

What other shape words can you name?
Shape words tell the shape of something or someone.
A rock might be any of these shapes.

a round rock
a flat rock
a pointed rock

A street might be one of these shapes.

a hilly street
a winding street
a crooked street

What other ways might a rock be shaped?
What other ways might a
street be shaped?

Words That Describe Color

Some words describe color. Here are a few color words.

red   golden   blue   gray
orange   reddish   pink   blond

Can you name other colors?

Color words tell the color of something.

orange pajamas
a blue car
reddish hair

What color is your shirt? What color are your socks? What color are your shoes?

Exercise   Describing Yourself

Copy this list on a sheet of paper.

               Me
_____ hair (color)
_____ nose (shape)
_____ eyes (color)
_____ fingers (size)
_____ front teeth (size)
_____ chin (shape)

216

Look at yourself in a mirror. Then, on each line, write a size, shape, or color word. Describe your hair, your nose, your eyes, your fingers, your front teeth, and your chin.

Groups of Words That Describe

Sometimes you need more than one size, shape, or color word. Here is an example.

a long, green caterpillar

The word *long* tells the caterpillar's size. The word *green* tells its color. Together, the words describe the caterpillar.

Here is another example.

the small, round sparrow

What word tells the sparrow's size? What word tells its shape?

Exercise Using Words That Describe

Copy the chart. Then fill in any two columns for each noun. Use words from the lists of size, shape, and color words, or write words of your own.

	Size	Shape	Color	Noun
1.	_____	_____	_____	apple
2.	_____	_____	_____	balloon
3.	_____	_____	_____	dandelion
4.	_____	_____	_____	freckle
5.	_____	_____	_____	worm
6.	_____	_____	_____	banana

When you finish, write each noun and the two words that describe it, such as *round, red apple.*

Part 2 Sentences That Describe

The picture shows a fishbowl. These two sentences describe the bowl.

1. The bowl has small white rocks.
2. It has thin green plants.

The first sentence tells the size and color of the rocks. The second sentence describes the shape and color of the plants.

Exercise Writing Sentences That Describe

Write two or more sentences about the fishbowl. Describe size, shape, or color in each sentence.

Part 3 Paragraphs That Describe

Sometimes it takes a whole paragraph to describe something. Here is an example.

The old bullfrog squatted on a rock. He was taking a sunbath. He was a giant water frog. He had webbed feet for swimming. A short while ago he had shed his skin. Now his new green coat was tight and shiny. The sun felt good on his new skin. —BERNIECE FRESCHET

Read the first sentence again. It is the topic sentence. It tells you that the paragraph is about a bullfrog.

The other sentences tell how the bullfrog looks. They use size, shape, and color words.

What word tells the size of the frog?
What word tells the shape of his feet?
What word tells the color of his new coat?

The paragraph paints a picture with words. The words help you to see the bullfrog in your mind.

Describing a Dragon

Read the paragraph. List the size, shape, and color words. Then study pictures 1, 2, and 3. Tell which picture shows the dragon that the paragraph describes.

The dragon was huge. It had a big head and long, white teeth. Its eyes were yellow. Its tiny ears were pointed. Down the middle of its curved back were red spikes. They went from its head to the end of its long tail.

Writing Paragraphs That Describe

Someday you may want to describe a person or thing in a paragraph. Here is one way to do it:

1. Start with a picture. It can be a picture in your mind. It can be a picture in front of you.

2. Study the picture. List words that describe it. Write size, shape, and color words.

3. Write a topic sentence. Name the person or thing. For example, here are three topic sentences.

> A catfish is a strange-looking fish.
> The dog looks old.
> The doll is beautiful.

4. Write three or four more sentences about your picture. Tell how the person or thing looks. Use size, shape, and color words.

5. Check and rewrite. Use these questions.

   a. Is the first line indented?
   b. Is each sentence complete?
   c. Does each sentence begin with a capital letter?
   d. Does each sentence end with a period?

Exercise   Writing a Paragraph That Describes

Choose one topic below. Draw a picture of it. Color your picture. Then write a description. Follow the five steps.

1. a rainbow	5. ear muffs for an elephant
2. a turtle	6. a ketchup bottle
3. a cloud	7. a dog sweater
4. a magic wand	8. the Beast with Ten Toes

Chapter 18

Getting Inside a Poem

Poems are full of mystery. Just as soon as you think you understand one perfectly, it changes. That's because poems grow when you read them. The more you put yourself into a poem, the more it will have to say.

Getting inside a poem means learning how it is put together. You need to live with a poem for a while. See how it makes you feel. When you feel comfortable with a poem, you know it is becoming part of you.

Part 1 Discovering the Shape of a Poem

A poem is different from a paragraph. Poets write in lines instead of sentences. In just a few words a poet says a lot. Each word in a poem is important.

Let's look now at a very short poem. It doesn't have a title.

The moon had
  a cat's mustache
For a second
      —JACK KEROUAC

The poet looks at the moon and sees something special. Not everyone has imagined a cat's mustache on the moon!

The poem has only one stanza. **Stanza** means a group of lines that go together.

Let's look at another poem that is one stanza long.

The Pumpkin Tide

I saw thousands of pumpkins last night
come floating in on the tide,
bumping up against the rocks and
rolling up on the beaches;
it must be Halloween in the sea.
      —RICHARD BRAUTIGAN

This poet also imagines something unusual. The poem is full of strong feeling.

Think about "The Pumpkin Tide." The idea of Halloween at sea may make you laugh.

The poet doesn't stop with laughter, though. He makes you feel the angry motion of the sea. The poem may remind you of storms when thousands of things wash up on the shore.

Read these lines aloud. What are the motion words?

bumping up against the rocks and
rolling up on the beaches;

Can you name all the things that you think about when you read this poem?

Now let's read a poem that has two stanzas.

City

In the morning the city
Spreads its wings
Making a song
In stone that sings.

In the evening the city
Goes to bed
Hanging lights
About its head.

—LANGSTON HUGHES

Each stanza in this poem has four lines. The last word in each line helps paint a picture. Some of these words rhyme.

In the first stanza, the poet describes the city in the morning. He compares the city to a bird.

The first stanza makes us feel the city taking off for a new day. We feel the energy of the city. The poet tells us the city is making a song. He wants us to have a happy feeling.

In the second stanza the poet talks about the city at night. He compares the city to a person going to bed.

The city is different from you and me, however. It doesn't sleep. Instead, it hangs lights around its head. What kind of feeling does the poet give you in this stanza?

You will find that poems come in all shapes. A poem may be short or long. It may rhyme or it may not. Some poets write in sentences. Others don't.

When you discover the shape of a poem, you begin to get inside it. Here are some guides that will help you get started.

Guides for Discovering the Shape of a Poem

1. Find the stanzas in the poem. Look for the idea or picture in each stanza.
2. Try to find the most important words in the poem.
3. Think about the feelings in the poem. What feelings does the poem give you?

Exercises Discovering the Shape of a Poem

A. Write a short poem. Arrange the words carefully. Make each line in your poem special. Choose one of the subjects below, or make up your own.

Bugs	Pancakes	Barefoot
Puppy	Beach	Dancing
December	Kitten	Flower

B. Exchange your poem with another person in your class. Now do these things.

1. Read the other person's poem to yourself.
2. Follow the guides above.
3. Read the poem out loud to your class.

Part 2   Seeing the Pictures in a Poem

You have seen that poets like to play with your imagination. They often paint pictures in words. They hope that the pictures will give you feelings.

Here's a poem that contains a picture.

Hokku

In the falling snow
A laughing boy holds out his palms
Until they are white.

—RICHARD WRIGHT

Can you draw this picture? You will need to include these things: falling snow, laughing boy, hands catching the snow.

What do you feel when you read this poem? Surely the snow on bare hands makes you feel cold. Do you think the boy's fingers sting? Why is he laughing?

Sometimes poets paint pictures to compare one thing with another. In Part 1 you read a poem called "City." There the poet compares the city to a bird.

Now let's look at another poem that makes a comparison. Here the poet compares trees in a storm to sweeping brooms.

Brooms

On stormy days
When the wind is high
Tall trees are brooms
Sweeping the sky.

They swish their branches
In buckets of rain,
And swash and sweep it
Blue again.

—DOROTHY ALDIS

In the first stanza, the poet says the trees are like brooms. In the second stanza, she shows the "brooms" at work.

What do the "brooms" do? How does the poem make you feel? Use very exact words when you talk about your feelings. Do you feel wet? Do your arms get tired when you think about all that sweeping?

Guides for Seeing Pictures in a Poem

1. Think about what the poet has put into the poem. Do the words make you think of something you have seen? Do they make you feel something you have felt before? Do they make you hear something you have heard before?

2. Think about whether the poet compares one thing to another. Does the poem make you see something in a new way? Does it give you a new feeling about something?

A. Read this poem. Then listen while your teacher reads it out loud. Talk about the poem in class. Follow the Guides for Seeing Pictures in a Poem.

Fog

The fog comes
   on little cat feet.

It sits looking
over harbor and city
on silent haunches
and then moves on.

—CARL SANDBURG

B. Write a short poem, three or four lines long. Your poem should paint a picture in words. Here are some ideas for poems. Choose one of them or make up your own.

Leaves Falling   A Storm at the Beach
Mowing the Grass   An Airplane Taking Off

C. Read your poem over. Follow the Guides for Seeing Pictures in a Poem. Is there anything you want to change in your poem? If there is, make the change. Be able to tell why you changed your poem.

Part 3 Hearing the Sounds in a Poem

Many poets play with sounds in their poems. In "City," the poet uses words that rhyme. In "Brooms," the poet uses lots of "s" sounds. Once in a while a poet will use a word that sounds like what it means. "Buzz" is a good example. When you read the word aloud, you hear the sound that bees make.

Let's begin to study sounds by looking more closely at rhyme.

Rhyme

Not all poems have rhymes, but many do. **Rhymes** are words that end with the same sound. For example, *hot* and *lot* are rhymes. *Wiggle* and *giggle* are rhymes.

As you read this poem, listen for rhymes.

Fred's Bed

Fred
uses his bed
for a sled,
and the floor below
for snow.

When his head bumps the floor,
it's not so nice:
the soft snow has turned
hard into ice.
Oh!

—EVE MERRIAM

In the first stanza, there are two sets of rhymes. They are *Fred, bed, sled* and *below, snow.*

Now look at the second stanza. It is easy to see that *nice* rhymes with *ice.* To find the word that rhymes with *Oh!,* you have to go back to the first stanza. There you will find *below* and *snow.*

Repeating Single Sounds

Remember the tongue-twister that goes like this?

She sells sea shells by the sea shore.

It's hard to say because of the *s* and *sh* sounds.

When a poet uses the same consonant sound over and over, we call it **alliteration.**

Sometimes poets use alliteration to help hold a poem together. The consonant sounds form a pattern. This pattern helps to give the poem shape.

Read the first stanza of this poem by Rhoda Bacmeister. Do you hear the alliteration of the *s* sound?

Galoshes
Susie's galoshes
Make splishes and sploshes
And slooshes and sloshes
As Susie steps slowly
Along in the slush.

What does the *s* sound make you think of?

Using Words that Sound Like What They Mean

Poets sometimes choose words that sound like what they mean. Here are some examples. Read them out loud.

buzz   gurgle   pop
scratch   snarl   flutter

Words that sound like what they mean are called **echoic.** Here is a line from a poem. Which words sound like what they mean?

The buzz-saw snarled and rattled in the yard.

What kind of feeling do these words give you?

Now read the guides below. They will help you remember what you have learned about sounds.

Guides for Hearing the Sounds in a Poem

1. Read your poem aloud. Listen for these special uses of sound.

    Rhyme—use of words that end with the same sound. Rhymes often come at the ends of lines.

    Alliteration—a pattern of consonant sounds

    Words that sound like what they mean

2. Think about how the sounds help you to understand the poem.

233

A. Read this poem. Then answer the questions in class.

Mrs. Peck-Pigeon

Mrs. Peck-Pigeon
Is picking for bread,
Bob-bob-bob
Goes her little round head.
Tame as a pussy cat
In the street,
Step-step-step
Go her little red feet.
With her little red feet
And her little round head,
Mrs. Peck-Pigeon
Goes picking for bread.

—ELEANOR FARJEON

1. Which words rhyme?
2. Which words sound like what they mean?

B. Here is the first stanza of a poem about a frog. The poem uses alliteration. Copy the stanza on your paper. Circle the words that begin with the same consonant sound.

The spotted frog
Sits quite still
On a wet stone

—VALERIE WORTH, "Frog"

Part 4   Feeling the Rhythm in a Poem

Many poems have a strong, regular beat. You can tap it out as you read. Listen while your teacher reads this poem about a swing.

The Swing

How do you like to go up in a swing,
    Up in the air so blue?
Oh, I do think it the pleasantest thing
    Ever a child can do!

Up in the air and over the wall,
    Till I can see so wide,
Rivers and trees and cattle and all
    Over the countryside—

Till I look down on the garden green,
    Down on the roof so brown—
Up in the air I go flying again,
    Up in the air and down!

        —ROBERT LOUIS STEVENSON

The poet has carefully arranged the beats. He captures the rhythm of swinging.

Marking the Beats

Look at the first stanza again. Let's put a mark over each strong beat.

235

How do you like to go úp in a swíng,
   Úp in the aír so blúe?
Óh, I do thínk it the pléasantest thíng
   Éver a chíld can dó!

Now read the first stanza out loud. Do you feel the motion of the swing?

Reading Aloud

When you read poems out loud, listen for the strong beat. Think about what the poem is saying. Let the rhythm and the meaning work together. Don't read in a sing-song way, but do let the poem's music become part of you.

> **Guides for Feeling the Rhythm in a Poem**
>
> 1. Read the poem aloud. Listen for the strong beats.
> 2. Think about the meaning of the poem.
> 3. Let the rhythm and the meaning work together.

Exercises   Feeling the Rhythm in a Poem

A. Here's another poem with a strong rhythm. Listen while your teacher reads it out loud.

Rope Rhyme

Gét set, réady now, júmp right ín
Bóunce and kíck and gíggle and spín

Listen to the rope when it hits the ground
Listen to that clappedy-slappedy sound
Jump right up when it tells you to
Come back down, whatever you do
Count to a hundred, count by ten
Start to count all over again
That's what jumping is all about
Get set, ready now,

        jump

         right

        out

—ELOISE GREENFIELD

There are four strong beats in each line. Can you hear them? Now your teacher will read the poem again. This time, clap out the strong beats.

B. Choose a poem with a strong rhythm. Follow the Guides for Feeling the Rhythm in a Poem. Practice reading the poem aloud several times before you read it in class.

Review Exercise   Getting Inside a Poem

Write a poem or a set of poems about anything you like. When you finish, think about each poem you have written. Ask yourself these questions.

   1. How did you shape your poem?
   2. Did you paint any pictures in your poem?
   3. What special sounds does your poem have?
   4. Does your poem have a strong rhythm? If
it does, mark the strongest beats.

237

Chapter 19

Making Friends with Books

Look at the picture on the opposite page. Where are the boys? What are they doing?

Books are like friends. They can teach you games. They can make you laugh. They can make you cry. They can make you afraid, just for a little while.

This chapter will help you to make new book-friends. It will teach you ways to share your new friends with others.

Part 1 Learning About Books

Every book has a name. It is called the **title.** The person who wrote the book is called the **author.**

Look at the picture below. Find the part of the book marked **spine.** The title is printed on the spine. The last name of the author is printed there, too.

Exercises Naming Titles and Authors

A. Here are three books. For each book, answer these two questions.

1. What is the title of the book?
2. What is the author's last name?

B. Imagine that you have written a book. It is about you. Make up a title for your book. Draw the outline of a book spine. Write the title on the spine. Then write your last name there, too.

Part 2 Finding Books

Do you like to cook? to play checkers? to paint pictures? to carve soap? to play baseball? to read mysteries? Whatever you like to do, the library has something for you.

To find books in the library, you need to know two important things.

1. The books for children are all in one place. They might be in a special room. They might be in a corner of a large room.

2. The books are arranged in a special way. All the storybooks are together. Books about the same things are also together. For example, books about plants are together. Books about the stars are together. Books about football players are together.

Exercises   Learning About the Library

A. Read the book titles in each group. Pick out the one book in each group that would *not* be with the others in the library.

1. *The Blue Lobster*
   Riddle Giggles
   Ants Have Pets
   Games Gorillas Play

2. *Metric Puzzles*
   The Three Wishes
   Peter Pan
   The Princess and the Pea

241

B. Go to the school or public library. You might want to ask the librarian to help you find these books.

1. one book about sports
2. one storybook
3. one book about plants
4. one book about pets

Write the title and author of each book.

Choosing Books

People you know can help you find good books. A librarian can show you books that you might like. Your teacher can suggest books. Your friends and older brothers and sisters can help, too. They can name books that they have enjoyed. A librarian can then help you find these books.

Another way to find books is to explore the library. Go to the children's section. Look at the books. Choose several. Page through them. Then decide on one or two.

Next, check your books out of the library. For this, you need a library card. A library card is free. When you have one, you can take out books at any time.

Do you have a library card? If not, ask a librarian to help you get one.

242 **Exercise   Choosing a Book**

Go to the library. Find two or three interesting books. Choose one and check it out.

Part 3 Reading a Book

Once in a while you probably get very interested in a book. You read wherever you can. You read in the morning, afternoon, and evening.

Many times, though, you probably forget to read. That is why you should set aside a time for reading every day. It can be in the morning. It can be after school or after dinner. It can be before bed.

You should also find a place to read. It should be quiet. It should have a comfortable chair. The chair should be in a place with good light. For daytime reading, the light can come from a window. For nighttime reading, it will come from a lamp.

Exercises Reading Your Book

A. Look at this picture. It shows a good reading place. Explain why it is good for reading.

B. Decide on a time and place for reading. Then read your library book.

Part 4 Sharing Books

You can share a good book with your classmates.
One way is to talk about the book. The picture below
shows two people. They are talking about a book.

I just finished a good book. The book is <u>The Man Who Took the Indoors Out</u>. It is by Arnold Lobel.

The title sounds interesting. What is the book about?

It is about a man named Bellwood Bouse. He invites all the things in his house to come outside. His furniture comes out. So does everything else. Later, Bellwood's things refuse to go back inside. The book is very funny. That is why I liked it.

I want to read it, too!

The boy told the girl four important things.

1. The title of the book
2. The author of the book
3. What the book is about
4. Why he liked the book

The boy shared the book with his friend.

244   Exercise   Talking About a Book

Share your book with a classmate. Tell about the four
important things listed above.

Writing About Books

You can share a book in another way. You can write a paragraph about it. Here is a paragraph about a book.

Dandelion by Ladislav Svatos explains how dandelions grow. It tells how the wind spreads dandelions seeds. It tells how the seeds grow into new dandelions. It describes their roots, leaves, and flowers. I liked this book because I learned many new things about dandelions.

The writer of the paragraph did four important things.

1. She gave the title of the book.
2. She named the author.
3. She told what the book is about.
4. She explained why she liked the book.

Exercise **Writing About a Book**

Write a paragraph about the book you read. Be sure your paragraph answers these questions.

1. What is the title?
2. Who is the author?
3. What is the book about?
4. Why did you like the book?

Chapter 20

Writing a Report

Do you like to go on trips? Have you ever gone on a trip with your class? Have you visited someplace special with your family? Have you gone to an interesting place with your friends?

Afterwards, you probably told someone about it. You talked about what you saw. This is one kind of report.

In this chapter you will study another kind of report. You will study *written* reports.

Part 1 What Is a Report?

A report is a group of paragraphs. The paragraphs give facts. The facts tell about a subject.

Some reports are short. They are only a few paragraphs. Other reports are long. They are many pages. In this chapter, the reports all have three paragraphs.

Here is a sample report.

Visiting a Farm

Last Saturday I visited my aunt and uncle. They live on a farm near Cornville. Their farm has large fields of corn and soybeans. Both crops are planted in long, straight rows.

My uncle showed me three huge machines. One was for planting seeds. One was for picking corn. Another was for picking soybeans.

My aunt showed me her garden. She grows tomatoes and beans. She also grows squash and watermelons.

The report tells about a farm. The report has three paragraphs. Each paragraph gives facts.

Paragraph 1 tells about the farm as a whole. It tells where the farm is located. It tells what crops are on the farm. It tells what the crops on the farm look like. The paragraph gives three facts.

1. The farm is near Cornville.
2. Corn and soybeans grow on the farm.
3. Corn and soybeans are planted in rows.

Paragraph 2 tells about the farm machines. It gives three facts.

1. One farm machine plants seeds.
2. One machine picks corn.
3. One machine picks soybeans.

Paragraph 3 tells about the garden. It gives two facts.

1. Tomatoes and beans grow in the garden.
2. Squash and watermelons grow in the garden.

Exercise Studying a Report

Read this report. Then answer the questions.

Our Visit to the Airport

Yesterday our class went to the airport. First, we saw the terminal. Travelers buy tickets and pick up baggage in this building. The terminal has places to sit and rest. It also has restaurants and shops.

We saw the control tower. There, workers direct planes in the air. They also direct planes on the ground. They tell pilots when to take off. They tell them when to land.

From the tower we saw the runway. White lines are painted down the center. Lines are painted along the sides, too. Planes take off and land on the runway.

1. What is the report about?
2. How many paragraphs does it have?
3. Which paragraph tells about the terminal?
4. Which paragraph tells about the runway?
5. Which paragraph tells about the control tower?
6. Write two facts from paragraph 1.
7. Write two facts from paragraph 2.
8. Write two facts from paragraph 3.

Part 2 Choosing a Subject

Many times your teacher gives you a subject. You then write about it. Sometime, though, you might have to choose a subject. Where do you begin?

First, make a list. Name interesting places you have visited. You might have visited the places with your class. You might have gone with your friends or with your family.

Here are some ideas.

a train station   a greenhouse
a fishing boat   a tree farm
another school   a post office
an amusement park   a police station
a cookie factory   a cheese factory

a zoo
a dairy
a forest
a museum
a pet shop

Next, look at your list. Circle the places you remember best. Then choose one for a report.

Exercise Deciding on a Subject   251

Choose a subject for your report. Follow the steps explained in the lesson. If you need help, ask your teacher.

Part 3   Making a Plan

You have a subject. Now you must plan your report.

Begin by thinking about your subject. Picture the place in your mind. Then list the important things you saw.

A Firehouse
outside of firehouse
fire trucks
special clothes
captain's desk
place where firefighters
* sleep and eat*

Choose three things to talk about. Circle them.

A Firehouse
outside of firehouse
(fire trucks)
(special clothes)
captain's desk
(place where firefighters
* sleep and eat)*

252   **Exercise   Beginning a Plan**

Think about the place you visited. List important things you saw. Circle three of them.

Making an Outline

An outline is a written plan. It tells the main ideas of a report. Here is an outline.

A Firehouse   **title**

  I. Fire trucks
 II. Special clothes   — **topics**
III. Place where firefighters sleep and eat

The **title** is *A Firehouse*. It names the subject. The first word in the title begins with a capital letter. It is **capitalized**. So are the other important words.

The outline has three **topics.** They name the main things to be covered in the report. They begin with capital letters.

Each topic is numbered with a Roman numeral. The numeral is followed by a period.

Exercises   Making Your Outline

A. Make an outline for your report. Name your subject in the title. Look at your list from the last exercise. Use the three circled things as your three topics.

B. Check your outline. Use these questions.

1. Is the first word in the title capitalized?
2. Are the other important words capitalized?
3. Does each topic have a Roman numeral?
4. Is each numeral followed by a period?
5. Is the first word in each topic capitalized?

Taking Notes

The next step is taking notes. Notes are groups of words. They help you to remember facts.

To take notes, divide a sheet of paper into three parts. At the top of each, write one topic from your outline.

Think about each topic. Think about what you saw. Write words to help you remember.

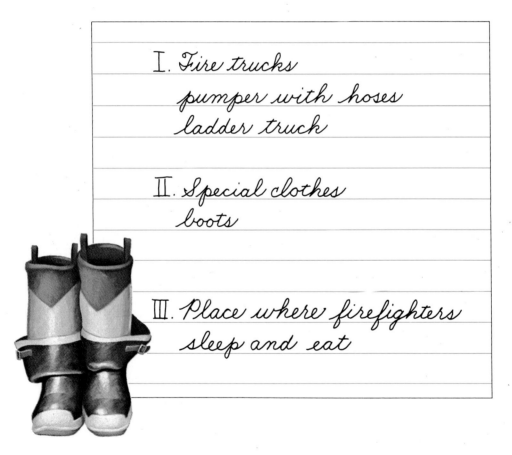

I. Fire trucks
   pumper with hoses
   ladder truck

II. Special clothes
    boots

III. Place where firefighters
     sleep and eat

Exercise   Writing Your Notes

Take notes for your report. Use your outline as a guide.

Part 4 Writing the Report

Next comes the writing of the report.

The First Sentence

The first sentence is important. It answers these questions.

> What?
> Who?
> When?

It can also answer this question.

> Where?

Here is a good first sentence.

> Last Wednesday our class
> visited the firehouse
> on Oak Street.

The sentence answers four questions.

> What? a firehouse
> Who? the class
> When? last Wednesday
> Where? Oak Street

The Rest of the Report

The rest of the report should follow the outline.
Each topic in the outline becomes a paragraph in the
report. The title of the outline becomes the title of
the report.

A Firehouse

Last Wednesday our class visited
the firehouse on Oak Street. We saw
two trucks. One was a pumper. It
had hoses for spraying water. The
other truck was a ladder truck.
It had tall ladders on top.

The firefighters showed us their
special clothes. They wear gloves, helmets,
and tall boots. They also wear heavy
coats. Sometimes they use masks.

The firefighters also showed us
where they sleep and eat. They
sleep in a big room. They cook their
meals in a tiny kitchen.

Exercise Writing Your Report

Write your report. First write a sentence that answers
the four questions. Then finish the report. Use your outline
and notes.

Part 5 Checking and Rewriting the Report

The last step is checking and rewriting the report. Use these guides.

Guides for Checking and Rewriting a Report

1. Does the report have a title?
2. Does the first word of the title begin with a capital letter?
3. Are the other important words capitalized?
4. Does the report have three paragraphs?
5. Is each paragraph indented?
6. Are all the sentences complete?
7. Does each sentence begin with a capital letter?
8. Does each sentence end with a period?

Correct any mistakes. Then make a final copy.

Exercise Finishing Your Report

Check your report. Rewrite anything you need to. Then make a neat copy.

Chapter 21

Writing Letters

Most of your friends go to your school. Others live in your neighborhood. Almost every day you talk with them. You and your friends share things that interest you.

Some friends may live far away from you. You may not get to talk with them often or for very long. Long-distance phone calls can be expensive. However, there is another good way to "talk" to someone far away. You can write a friendly letter. If you write an interesting letter, your friend will want to write back. Even though you are not together, you and your friend can share things.

Part 1 Writing a Friendly Letter

The most important part of a friendly letter is the message. Your news for your friend is the reason you are writing. However, there are other parts in a friendly letter, also. These other parts give your friend information he or she needs to understand the message. For example, your friend needs to know who wrote the letter. In all, there are five parts in a friendly letter. Look at the sample letter on page 261. Then read about the five parts.

Keep your letter easy to read. You may use printing or cursive writing. Choose the way that will be clearer to your friend.

Heading

The heading tells where you are when you write the letter. It tells what day you are writing the letter.

If you are at home, your heading is your home address. Write your house number and street name on the first line. Write your city, state, and ZIP code number on the second line. If you are on a trip or at camp, write the address where you are staying.

Under your address, write the date. Your friend will want to know when you wrote the letter.

Look at the heading on the sample letter. Notice where the heading is placed. The lines of the heading begin at about the middle of the paper. All three begin at the same place.

Sample Friendly Letter

1748 Wharton Drive

Heading   Cleveland, Ohio 44101

March 14, 1981

Dear Bill,   **Greeting**

     I still have my stamp collection. Now it is almost as big as your collection. Yesterday I went to the post office and bought some new wildlife stamps. **Message** Three stamps have water birds on them and two have forest animals. Maybe we could trade stamps through the mail. If you like, I'll send you a list of my stamps.

Closing   Your friend,

Signature   Sam

Greeting

The greeting is the way you say "hello" in a letter. Here are some different greetings you could use.

Dear Ann,   *Hi, Ann,*   *Hello, Ann,*

Read the greeting in the sample letter. See where it is placed. It is on a line by itself. Skip a line between the heading and the greeting. The greeting begins near the left edge of the paper. Remember to leave a margin between the edge of the paper and your writing.

Body

The body of the letter is your message. Write about things your friend will be interested in. Show interest in what your friend is doing, too.

Write your ideas in sentences. Put capital letters, periods, and other punctuation marks where they belong. Except for the first line, begin all the lines in the body at the same place you began your greeting. Keep your margin straight.

Indent the first line of the body. This means to leave some space at the beginning of the line. Notice where the body of the sample letter begins. Remember that the body never begins on the same line as the greeting.

If your letter is long, you may need to break it into paragraphs. All the sentences in one paragraph should be about the same subject. When you start telling about a new subject, start a new paragraph. You do this by indenting the first line of the new paragraph.

Closing

The closing is the part of the letter where you say "goodbye." Here are some different closings.

Your friend,   Sincerely,   Yours truly,

Always begin your closing with a capital letter. If the closing has two words, do not use a capital letter in the second word. Use a comma after the closing.

Find the closing on the sample letter. Notice that it is lined up under the greeting. It begins at about the middle of the paper. Skip a line between the body and the closing.

Signature

The signature is your name. If you are writing to a close friend, your first name is probably enough. However, your friend may know other people with the same name. Then it would be good to write your whole name. If you are not sure, use your whole name.

Find the signature on the sample letter. Notice that it begins at the same place as the closing.

Exercises Writing a Friendly Letter

A. Number your paper from 1 to 5. Match each part of a friendly letter with the sample of that part. After the number of the part, write the letter of the sample.

1. heading
2. greeting
3. message
4. closing
5. signature

A.   Today was exciting! A team from a TV station visited our school. They took pictures. My class was on the 6:00 news!

B. Valerie

C. Hi, Jamie,

D. Your cousin,

E. 543 Oakton Avenue
Ames, Iowa 50010
April 1, 1981

B. Use the sample parts of a letter from Exercise A. Put them in the correct order. Write the parts on your paper in the correct places for a letter.

C. Write a friendly letter to a friend of yours. Use your real address in the heading. You may tell about a real thing that has happened to you. You may write about an imaginary happening. Remember to write all the parts of the letter in the correct places.

Part 2 Addressing an Envelope

The envelope will protect your letter. It will also make sure that the letter is delivered safely. Many workers at the post office must read what you write on the envelope. Everything must be correct and in the right place. Then your friend will get the letter quickly.

Every envelope needs three things. They are an address, a return address, and a postage stamp. Before you write on your envelope, make sure it is right-side up. The flap should open at the top.

Look at the sample envelope below. Then read about the three things an envelope needs.

Sample Envelope

Carla Wilson
625 King Road
Boston, Massachusetts
02156

Return address

Postage stamp

Your friend's name and address

Miss Sarah Collins
4513 Grove Street
Detroit, Michigan 48112

The Address

The address tells where the letter should go. It has three lines.

On the first line, write the name of your friend. Be sure to use both the first name and the last name. If you are writing to an adult it is polite to write a title before your friend's name. You would use one of these titles.

Mr.   Use this title for any man.
Ms.   Use this title for any woman.
Miss   Use this title if the woman is not married.
Mrs.   Use this title if the woman is married.

If you are writing to a young person, use a title if you like. Notice that there are periods after *Mr., Ms.,* and *Mrs.* Do not use a period after *Miss* in a title.

On the second line, write your friend's house number and the name or number of the street.

On the third line, write the city and the state your friend lives in. Then write the ZIP code number. If there is not enough space on the third line, the ZIP code number may go on a separate line below the state name.

Look at the address on the sample envelope. See where it is placed. Begin the first line about half-way down the envelope, and almost half-way across. Begin the next two lines directly under the first line.

When you are finished, check your writing. Make sure the numbers are correct and clear.

The Return Address

The return address is your own address. It is needed in case there is a problem with delivery. Perhaps your friend moved, and is not at the address you used. Perhaps the address you wrote has a mistake in it. Then the post office may have to return the letter to you. That is why your own address is called the *return address*.

The return address has three lines, just like the address for your friend. Follow the same directions. Notice, however, where the return address is placed. You will find the return address in the upper left-hand corner of the sample envelope on page 265.

The Postage Stamp

Place the postage stamp in the upper right-hand corner of your envelope. Be careful if your letter is very heavy. It may need more stamps than a regular letter does. Go to a post office if you are not sure. There a postal worker will weigh your letter. He or she will tell you the right amount of postage.

Exercises   Addressing an Envelope

A. Copy this picture on your paper. Fill in the boxes with the correct number.

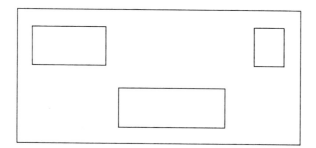

1. Address   3. Postage stamp
2. Return address

B. On your paper, draw a rectangle as big as a real envelope. Address this envelope to your teacher at the school address. Write your own address as the return address. Draw a stamp.

C. On your paper, draw another rectangle as big as a real envelope. Address this envelope to a friend or a relative. Write your own address as the return address. Draw a stamp.

Part 3   Writing Notes

A note is a short letter. You should know how to write three kinds of notes. They are invitations, answers to invitations, and thank-you notes.

Notes have five parts, just like letters. However, sometimes the heading is shorter than usual. It may use only the date.

Invitations

In an invitation, you invite someone to a special event. The event may be a birthday party at your house. It may be a program at school. Your invitation must be clear and exact. It must give the following information.

1. What is the event? If it is a party, be sure to tell what kind of party.
2. When is the event? Tell the day and time.
3. Where is the event? Tell the address.

February 20, 1981

Dear Maria,

What   Please come to my eighth
birthday party. It will be from
When
noon to two o'clock on Saturday,
March 7. We will be having a
cookout. The party will be at
Where
my house, 478 Beechwood. I
hope you can be there and
join the fun.

Your friend,
Susie Cheng

Answers to Invitations

Suppose you have a party. How much food should you buy? How much fruit drink will you need? You cannot make plans until you know who is coming. That is why answers to invitations are so important.

Before you answer an invitation, be sure of your answer. Do not change your mind later.

Your answer should tell whether you are coming. If you cannot come, it is polite to give a reason.

February 25, 1981

Dear Susie,
    Your cookout party should be fun. I'll be glad to come.

        Your friend,
        Maria Fernandez

February 25, 1981

Dear Susie,
    Thank you for the party invitation. I won't be able to come on Saturday because my family is going on a trip. I'm sorry that I will have to miss the party. I hope you have a very nice birthday.

        Your friend,
        Jeff Sutton

Thank-You Notes

You like someone to thank you when you do something nice. Other people feel the same way. A thank-you note shows that you like what someone did for you.

Here are some times you may want to write thank-you notes.

1. You receive a gift.
2. You stay at a friend's house overnight.
3. Someone does a special favor for you, like feeding your cat while you are on vacation.

In your thank-you note, say exactly what you are thankful for. Also, say something nice about the gift or favor. Let the person know the good things you are thinking about the gift or favor.

September 5, 1981

Dear Aunt Meg and Uncle Steve,
I've been telling all my
friends about my visit to your
farm. I miss hearing the
rooster crow in the morning.
My alarm clock doesn't sound
as friendly. Thank you for
inviting me. I had lots of fun.

Your nephew,
Cliff

Exercises   Writing Notes

A. Imagine that you are having a party at your home. Write an invitation to your party. Include all five parts of a note. For your greeting, use *Dear Classmate.* Give all the needed information.

B. Exchange the invitations you wrote for Exercise A with a classmate. First, write a "yes" answer to your classmate's invitation. Second, write a "no" answer. Give a reason.

273

C. Imagine that you received a pet dragon for your birthday. Write a thank-you note for the gift.

Chapter 22

Using Capital Letters

In both printing and cursive writing, there are
capital letters.

A B C D

a B C D

Capital letters have several important uses. Knowing
these uses will help you in two ways. First, you will
better understand what you read. Second, you will
know how to use capital letters correctly in your own
writing. This will help your readers understand what
you have written.

Part 1 Names of People and Pets

Using a capital letter to begin a word is called **capitalizing** the word. We capitalize special words. A person's name is a special word. A pet's name is a special word. Capitalize those names.

Mary   Robert   Muffin

> Begin the name of every person or pet with a capital letter.

A name may have more than one word. Use a capital letter to begin each word in a name.

Mary McLeod Bethune   Robert Edward Lee

Initials

People often write only the first letter of a name. That first letter stands for the whole name. It is called an **initial.** Always use a capital letter for an initial. Use a period after the initial.

Mary M. Bethune   Robert E. Lee

> Use capital letters for initials.
>
> Use a period after every initial.

Titles

Many names have titles in them. A title is part of a name. Therefore, a title is capitalized.

Here is a list of titles used often. After each title is the short form of that title.

Mister	Mr.
Mistress	Mrs.
Miss	_____ (no short form)
_____ (no long form)	Ms.
Doctor	Dr.

The short form of a word is called an **abbreviation.** Use a period after each abbreviation. Capitalize an abbreviation of a title.

Mrs. Cunningham   Mr. Gomez

Capitalize a title in a name.

Capitalize abbreviations of titles.

The Word *I*

The word *I* is used in place of a name. It is always capitalized.

Capitalize the word *I.*

A. Copy these names. Use capital letters where they are needed.

1. luke skywalker
2. mr. evans
3. susan b. anthony
4. dr. mitchell
5. conchita

6. martin luther king
7. miss stern
8. charlie brown
9. lassie
10. thomas a. edison

B. Follow the directions for Exercise A.

1. dr. wong
2. john f. kennedy
3. mrs. barton
4. ms. morrow
5. donald duck

6. minnie mouse
7. john paul jones
8. mr. spock
9. mary mapes dodge
10. cinderella

C. Copy these sentences. Use capital letters correctly.

1. The first woman doctor was elizabeth blackwell.
2. My friends tomoko and julie walk to school.
3. May i have two hamburgers?
4. Harriet tubman was a brave woman.
5. Mrs. antoni came from Italy.
6. The man in black clothes is darth vader.
7. I rode my bike with marcy.
8. John philip sousa wrote marches.
9. Dr. stein cleaned my teeth.
10. Our mailman is mr. kaplan.

Part 2 Names of Particular Places and Things

Names of particular places and things are special. Like names of people and pets, they are capitalized.

Tampa, Florida   Pepsi   New Year's Day

Many names of this sort have more than one word. Capitalize every important word in the name. You do not capitalize little words such as *a, the,* or *of.*

Big Mac   the Fourth of July

> Capitalize every important word in the name of a special place or thing.

These four groups of names must be capitalized.

1. Capitalize names of days, months, holidays, and other special days. Also, capitalize abbreviations for days and months.

Sunday	May	Memorial Day
Monday	June	Thanksgiving
Tues.	Oct.	Halloween
Wed.	Nov.	Columbus Day

2. Capitalize names of special buildings.

the White House   Union School

3. Capitalize names of streets and roads. Also, capitalize abbreviations of streets and roads.

Randolph Road   Randolph Rd.
Lake Avenue   Lake Ave.
South 4th Street   So. 4th St.

4. Capitalize names of towns, cities, states, and countries.

Carbondale, Illinois   Canada
Kansas City, Kansas   Mexico

Some names for groups of people are made from the names of places. Capitalize those names.

Canada — Canadians   Mexico — Mexicans
America — Americans   Italy — Italians

Exercises Using Capital Letters for Names of Particular Places and Things

A. Copy these names of places and things. Use capital letters where they are needed.

1. midpark school
2. united states of america
3. maple street
4. florida
5. denver
6. sunday
7. memorial day
8. ohio
9. february
10. ridge road

280 **B.** Copy these sentences. Use capital letters correctly.

1. Today is tuesday, july 15.
2. Laura visited phoenix, arizona.

3. The shoe store is on state street.
4. Have you ever visited mexico?
5. Bonita goes to hazeldell school.
6. We saw fireworks on the fourth of july.
7. I live on richmond road.
8. Columbus was an italian.
9. We celebrate thanksgiving in november.
10. Mom works in the webster building.

Part 3 First Words

Names of people, places, or things are capitalized wherever they are written. Other words are capitalized if they are used in particular places in writing. Here are five rules for using capital letters.

1. Capitalize the first word of every sentence.

This program is funny.	Declarative
Do you watch it often?	Interrogative
Please turn up the sound.	Command
How silly the story is!	Exclamation

2. Capitalize the first word of a quotation. A **quotation** means the exact words a person says. **Quotation marks** (" ") show the beginning and ending of a quotation.

Louisa asked, "May I help?"
(The quotation is "May I help?")
"Yes, thank you," said Fred.
(The quotation is "Yes, thank you.")

3. In most poems, capitalize the first word in every line.
The new line may begin in the middle of a sentence. Use a capital letter anyway. Notice how capital letters are used in this poem.

> One day a funny kind of man
> Came walking down the street.
> He wore a shoe upon his head,
> And hats upon his feet.
> —NATALIE JOAN, "A Funny Man"

4. Capitalize the first word in the greeting and in the closing of a letter.
The **greeting** is at the beginning of the letter.

> Dear Jean,   Hi, Ed,

The **closing** is at the end of the letter.

> Sincerely,   Yours truly,

5. Capitalize the first word of each idea in an outline.
An **outline** is a list of important ideas. You may make an outline to help you remember what you learn. You may make an outline to help you decide what to write in a report.

> Animals of the Far North
> I. Huskies
> II. Polar Bears
> III. Walrus

282

Notice that Roman numerals are used to number the ideas in the outline.

Exercises Using Capital Letters for First Words

A. Copy these sentences, quotations, poem, and letter. Use capital letters where they are needed.

1. this apple pie is good.
2. angela said, "it's my turn now."
3. "wear your mittens," said joe.
4. grandmother listens to the news.
5. elephants like peanuts.
6. the skier raced down the hill.
7. behold the duck.
   it does not cluck.
   a cluck it lacks.
   it quacks.
   —OGDEN NASH, "The Duck"
8. dear brian,
   i hope you can come to my birthday party. we are going to a movie. then we will have hot dogs and cake at my house. it will really be fun. i'll see you soon.

   your friend,
   betsy

B. Copy these sentences. Use capital letters correctly.

1. sometimes clouds look like pictures.
2. carla shouted, "try to catch me!"
3. mom asked, "would you like some popcorn?"
4. the mouse ran under the chair.
5. monster movies scare me.
6. "wait for me," said kelly.

Part 4   Titles

Capitalize most of the words in titles of TV
programs, movies, books, or other writings. You
always capitalize the first and last words. Also,
capitalize every important word. The only words you
should not capitalize in titles are little ones like *and,
of, in,* and *the.* Capitalize these only if they come first.

The Story of Ping   *Where the Wild*
Madeline and the Bad Hat   *Things Are*

> Capitalize the first, last, and every other important
> word in a title.

Notice the kind of print used in the samples above.
This is called **italic** print. It is used to set off titles of
books. You do not write italic letters. When you write
the title of a book, underline the words in the title.

Where the Wild Things Are

Do not underline the titles of short writings
like stories, poems, or reports. Use quotation marks
around these titles.

"Snow White and the Seven Dwarfs"
"The Pied Piper"
"Animals of the Far North"

Exercises   Using Capital Letters in Titles

A. Copy these titles. Use capital letters where they are needed. Copy the quotation marks and underlining shown.

1. mary poppins
2. "little snail"
3. walter the lazy mouse
4. "the swing"
5. "teach your dog tricks"
6. pippi longstocking
7. "flowers of the forest"
8. the bear scouts
9. space cat
10. the wizard of oz

B. Follow the directions for Exercise A.

1. "little red riding hood"
2. my father's dragon
3. "boats sail on the rivers"
4. "goldilocks and the three bears"
5. the cat in the hat
6. "my shadow"
7. "the reason for the pelican"
8. the last battle
9. "the gingerbread man"
10. make way for ducklings

More Exercises

Using Capital Letters

A. Using Capital Letters for Names of People and Pets, and I (Use after page 277.)

Copy these sentences. Use capital letters where they are needed.

1. The first man on the moon was neil armstrong.
2. This story is about a horse named flicka.
3. Penny and i won the race.
4. My favorite writer is dr. seuss.
5. This letter is from ms. kelly.
6. The head coach is mr. johnson.
7. Today i hit a home run.
8. My kitten is called fluffy.
9. Those tulips were drawn by rosa.
10. A. a. milne wrote about winnie-the-pooh.

B. Using Capital Letters for Names of Particular Places and Things (Use after page 280.)

Copy these names of places and things. Use capital letters where they are needed.

1. oxford elementary school
2. grand canyon
3. park avenue
4. mothers' day
5. madison public library
6. france
7. tuesday
8. april
9. main st.
10. africans

C. Using Capital Letters for First Words
(Use after page 282.)

Copy the sentences, quotations, poem, and letter. Use capital letters where they are needed.

1. do not feed the bears.
2. mrs. rice said, "those berries are ripe."
3. wool comes from sheep.
4. george said, "i cannot tell a lie."
5. is a caterpillar ticklish?
   well, it's always my belief
   that he giggles, as he wiggles
   across a hairy leaf.
   > —MONICA SHANNON,
   > "Only My Opinion"
6. dear larry,
   today our class went to the cleveland
   museum of art. we saw paintings and other
   things. i liked the african masks the best.
   > sincerely,
   > hector

D. Using Capital Letters in Titles   (Use after page 284.)

Copy these titles. Use capital letters where they are needed. Copy the quotation marks and underlining.

1. harry, the dirty dog
2. "the three little pigs"
3. "magic tricks you can learn"
4. the giants' farm
5. "the elephant's child"
6. bread and jam for frances

Chapter 23

Using Punctuation Marks

Punctuation marks are the marks used in writing. Some of them are the period (.), the question mark (?), the exclamation point (!) and the comma (,). These marks show where sentences end. They separate ideas. They point out questions and other types of sentences. They help you understand writing.

Study these explanations of punctuation marks. Use punctuation marks correctly in your writing. Then people who read your writing will understand your writing better.

Part 1 The Period

A period looks like this. ·

A period is used in several different places in writing. It is usually a clue that something has ended.

1. Use a period at the end of a statement or a command.

Statements   I like scary stories.
               Sam tells stories well.

Commands   Turn off the lights.
              Talk in a whisper.

The period tells you the sentence has ended. If you read the sentence aloud, your voice goes down at the end.

2. Use a period after an initial.

Martha D. Washington   E. B. White

The period tells that the single letter stands for a whole name.

3. Use a period after most abbreviations. Days, months, streets, titles in names, and other words have abbreviations. Here are some examples.

inch	in.	cup	c.
foot	ft.	ounce	oz.
yard	yd.	pint	pt.
mile	mi.	quart	qt.
pound	lb.	gallon	gal.

street	st. ✓	Company	Co. ✓
road	rd. ✓	Post Office	P.O. ✓
avenue	ave. ✓	Junior	Jr. ✓
Doctor	Dr. ✓	Mister	Mr. ✓
(no long form)	Ms. ✓	Mistress	Mrs. ✓

Some abbreviations do not need periods. Here are some abbreviations that do not use periods.

gram	g	Zone Improvement Plan	ZIP
meter	m	National Broadcasting	
liter	l	Company	NBC

Exercises   Using the Period Correctly

A. Copy the following word groups, or phrases. Use periods where they are needed.

1. Oct 31
2. U S Grant
3. The Marshall Co
4. 6 lbs
5. Dr Parker
6. Wed , Feb 2
7. P O Box 16
8. Mayfield Rd
9. Ms Carter
10. 4 oz

B. Copy the following sentences. Use periods where they are needed.

1. Close the window
2. Mr Nimitz lives next door
3. The pudding needs one quart of milk
4. The drug store is on Fifth Street
5. Ms Kelly drives a small, red car

6. Read the directions
7. Turn left at the corner
8. Mrs Harris is my teacher

Part 2   The Question Mark

A question mark looks like this.   ?

It is used at the end of every question.

> Are you going for a walk?
> May I come, too?

If you read these sentences aloud, your voice goes up at the end.

Exercise   Using the Question Mark Correctly

Copy the following sentences. Some are statements. Some are commands. Some are questions. Use the correct ending mark at the end of each sentence.

1. What is your name
2. Will you play with me
3. I am eight years old
4. Do you see the North Star
5. Ronald stood on his head
6. How tall is that horse
7. Take your turn
8. Does Karen like peanuts
9. Add these numbers
10. Has Joel ever visited a museum

Part 3 The Exclamation Point

An exclamation point looks like this. $\boxed{!}$

It is used at the end of exclamations. It shows surprise, anger, fright, or other strong feeling.

> How cold this water is! ⁄
> Don't splash me! ⁄
> I can't swim! ⁄
> Let's race! ⁄

If you read an exclamation aloud, try to show feeling in your voice.

Exercise Using the Exclamation Correctly

Copy the following sentences. All four kinds are mixed together. Use the correct ending mark at the end of each sentence. Be able to read each of the sentences with meaning. Your voice should let your listeners know what kind each sentence is.

1. Tulips grow in the spring
2. The house is on fire
3. When will the movie begin
4. What a huge ant that is
5. Jack made a sand castle
6. Read the poem aloud
7. Bring your ball to the picnic
8. How dangerous that stunt is
9. How do you feel today
10. Kia can roller skate

Part 4   The Comma

A comma looks like this. $\boxed{,}$

It is used in several places in writing. If you are reading aloud, it is a clue that you stop briefly at that place in the sentence. It is not an ending mark. It simply separates ideas or sentence parts that go together.

1. In writing dates, use a comma between the day and the year.

> July 4, 1776
> The war ended on November 11, 1918.

2. In writing addresses, use a comma between the city and the state.

> Atlanta, Georgia
> Indians built their homes in caves at Mesa
>   Verde, Colorado.

3. In a series of three or more persons or things, use a comma to separate them.

> The children wore heavy jackets,⁽¹⁾
>   woolen scarves,⁽²⁾ and warm gloves.⁽³⁾

> The singers are Ann,⁽¹⁾ Eddie,⁽²⁾ and Valerie.⁽³⁾

A series must have three or more parts.

Exercise   Using Commas

Copy the following sentences. Use commas where they are needed.

1. Send the letter to Dallas Texas.
2. Dolores Shari and Joy will come with me.
3. Our country began on July 4 1776.
4. My aunt lives in Chicago Illinois.
5. Al ate soup a sandwich and some cookies.
6. This bus goes to Denver Colorado.
7. Kip Chris and Pat played jump rope.
8. Mrs. Miller was born on May 4 1950.
9. The movie opened on December 7 1979.
10. Los Angeles California is a big city.

4. In a friendly letter, use a comma after the greeting and after the closing.

Sample Greetings

Dear Frank,   *Dear Ms. Silver,*

Sample Closings

Sincerely,   *Yours truly,*

5. Use a comma to set off a direct quotation from the rest of the sentence. A direct quotation means the exact words a person says. Usually, a sentence also tells who said the words. The comma comes between the quotation and that other part of the sentence.

295

Gloria said, "It's almost lunchtime."
The comma comes between *Gloria said* and
the words she said.

"I have a peanut butter sandwich," Joe said.
The comma comes between what Joe said
and the words *Joe said*.

Place the comma before the quotation marks.

6. Use a comma after *yes* or *no* at the beginning of a sentence.

Yes, the answer is 143.
No, New Orleans does not get much snow.

7. Use a comma after the name of the person spoken to.

Gerry, I found your pencil case.
Kumi, can you skate?

Exercises   Using the Comma Correctly

A. Copy the following sentences. Use commas where
they are needed.

1. Yes I would like some milk.
2. Tran will you help me?
3. Mother said "Be home for lunch."
4. Mr. Parker grows daisies roses and tulips.
5. "I can swim three laps" Gina said.
6. Fred comes from Detroit Michigan.
7. No I forgot my mitt.
8. Grandpa said "Watch how I do this."

B. Copy the following letter. Use commas correctly.

Dear Penny

    Yesterday I went on a nature walk with my class. We collected leaves from maples oaks and elms. Our teacher said "Watch out for poison ivy." Leaf collecting is exciting. Yes I had a good time.

Yours truly
Meg

Part 5 The Apostrophe

The apostrophe looks like this.   `'`

The apostrophe has two important uses.

1. Use an apostrophe in possessive nouns.

To make a singular noun show possession, add an apostrophe and an *s*.

Kathy's dog   Mark's marbles
the girl's pet   the boy's game

If a plural noun does not end in *s*, add an apostrophe and an *s* to show possession.

the women's department   the men's shoe store

If a plural noun ends in *s*, add only an apostrophe.

the painters' brushes   the bears' dens

2. Use an apostrophe in contractions. A contraction is a word formed by putting together two words. Some letters of the original words are left out. The apostrophe shows where letters are left out.

I am	I'm	is not	isn't
you are	you're	can not	can't
he is	he's	should not	shouldn't
she will	she'll	have not	haven't
it is	it's	has not	hasn't
they are	they're	do not	don't

The contraction for *will not* is *won't*.

Exercises   Using the Apostrophe Correctly

A. Copy the following phrases. Use apostrophes correctly to make every underlined noun show possession.

1. <u>Albertos</u> house
2. a <u>flys</u> buzz
3. all <u>foxes</u> tails
4. <u>Dianes</u> kitten
5. a <u>wizards</u> cape
6. <u>Mothers</u> job
7. the <u>horses</u> manes
8. the <u>kittens</u> tail
9. a <u>referees</u> whistle
10. <u>childrens</u> voices

B. Change each of the following phrases to a contraction. Write it on your paper.

1. can not
2. I will
3. you are
4. would not
5. he is
6. she will
7. you would
8. I would
9. will not
10. we are

Part 6   Quotation Marks

Quotation marks look like this.   " "

Quotation marks have two important uses.

1. Use quotation marks to set off direct quotations. Use one set of quotation marks before the exact words a person says. Use another set of quotation marks after the words.

"The dinosaur was the largest animal," Dan said.
Louise asked, "What did dinosaurs eat?"

In addition to quotation marks, a comma sets off a direct quotation. Read the sample sentences again. Notice that the quotation marks come after the comma.

2. Use quotation marks around titles of poems, stories, and reports.

"Simple Simon" "Cinderella" "All About Lions"

Exercise   Using Quotation Marks Correctly

Copy the following sentences. Use quotation marks where they are needed.

1. This rock is sandstone, said Miss Thomas.
2. Terence said, The soup is too hot.
3. Carol asked, Have you heard this joke?
4. Goldilocks and the Three Bears is a fairy tale.
5. The poem Paul Revere's Ride tells a story.
6. Do you know the story called Sleeping Beauty?

299

7. I'll water the flowers, said Toru.
8. The Animal Fair is a funny poem.
9. The conductor said, All aboard!
10. I want a hamburger, said Rita.

Part 7 Underlining

Underline titles of books. Remember to follow the rules for capitalizing words in titles.

The 500 Hats of Bartholomew Cubbins

In books, these titles are printed in italic letters.

The 500 Hats of Bartholomew Cubbins

Exercise Using Underlining Correctly

Copy these titles. Use quotation marks or underlining correctly.

Sample Question 1 The Sun (book)

Answer The Sun

Sample Question 2 Jabberwocky (poem)

Answer "Jabberwocky"

1. Homer Price (book)
2. Three Jolly Huntsmen (poem)
3. Ghostly Folktales (book)
4. The Camel (poem)
5. Windy Nights (poem)
6. The Hungry Thing (book)

More Exercises

Using Punctuation Marks

A. Using the Period Correctly   (Use after page 291.)

Copy the following word groups, or phrases. Use periods where they are needed.

1. Mr Chen
2. Aug 18
3. 1 ft 2 in
4. Erie Blvd
5. P O Box 53
6. p 47
7. Springfield Shoelace Co
8. Joseph Addison, Jr
9. Mrs Jackson
10. E Ninth St

B. Using the Question Mark Correctly
(Use after page 292.)

Copy the following sentences. Some are statements. Some are commands. Some are questions. Use the correct ending mark at the end of each sentence.

1. Can you count to one thousand
2. Barbara wished on a star
3. Where is your telephone
4. Please turn off the TV
5. The snake shed its skin
6. Do you hear a siren
7. Did you see an ambulance
8. We went on a picnic
9. Pick the red tomatoes
10. What day is your birthday

C. Using the Exclamation Point Correctly
(Use after page 293.)

Copy the following sentences. All four kinds are mixed together. Use the correct ending mark at the end of each sentence.

1. Three big dogs are fighting in my yard
2. Dad rides a bus to work
3. How bright the stars are tonight
4. Please sit on the sofa
5. Can you read that sign
6. What a hard test that was
7. Clouds hid the sun
8. Where is the fire station
9. Be sure to lock the door
10. Don't drop that dish

D. Using the Comma Correctly   (Use after page 296.)

Copy the following letter. Use commas where they are needed.

Dear Grandpa
    Mom and I looked at the stars last night. They were beautiful! I said "I can see the Big Dipper and the North Star." We even saw the Milky Way. Grandpa do you ever look at stars?

                                        Love
                                        Heather

E. Using the Apostrophe Correctly (Use after page 298.)

Copy each sentence. Change each underlined word or phrase to either a possessive or a contraction.

1. The washing machine will not work.
2. This is Juanitas house.
3. The monsters eyes were yellow.
4. You are my best friend.
5. The goose would not help the red hen.
6. You are not ever late for school.

F. Using Quotation Marks Correctly
(Use after page 299.)

Copy the following sentences. Use quotation marks where they are needed.

1. The sand is hot! said Luis.
2. Todd said, Are you ready?
3. Maria read The Brave Little Tailor.
4. Kent likes the poem Eletelephony.
5. Dorothy said, I want to go home.
6. Hansel and Gretel is a good fairy tale.

G. Using Underlining Correctly (Use after page 300.)

Copy these titles. Use quotation marks or underlining.

1. Caps for Sale (book)
2. The Real Princess (story)
3. Green Eggs and Ham (book)
4. The Grasshopper (poem)
5. The Moon (book)
6. The Horse and His Boy (book)

303

Index

Acknowledgments

A. S. Barnes & Company, Inc: For "A Funny Man" by Natalie Joan from *Barnes Book of Nursery Verse*, compiled by Barbara Ireson; © 1960 by A. S. Barnes & Company; all rights reserved. City Lights Books: For "The moon had" from *Scattered Poems* by Jack Kerouac; copyright © 1970, 1971 by The Estate of Jack Kerouac. Thomas Y. Crowell, Publishers: For "Rope Rhyme" from *Honey, I Love and Other Love Poems* by Eloise Greenfield; copyright © 1978 by Eloise Greenfield. Delacorte Press/Seymour Lawrence: For "The Pumpkin Tide" excerpted from the book *The Pill Versus The Springhill Mine Disaster* by Richard Brautigan; copyright © 1968 by Richard Brautigan. Doubleday & Company, Inc.: For "Only My Opinion" from the book *Goose Grass Rhymes* by Monica Shannon; copyright 1930 by Doubleday & Company, Inc. E. P. Dutton & Co., Inc.: For "Galoshes" from *Stories to Begin On* by Rhoda W. Bacmeister; copyright 1940 by E. P. Dutton & Co., Inc.; renewal copyright 1968 by Rhoda W. Bacmeister. Farrar, Straus & Giroux, Inc.: For "Frog" from *Small Poems* by Valerie Worth, pictures by Natalie Babbit; copyright © 1972 by Valerie Worth. Harcourt Brace Jovanovich, Inc.: For "Fog" from *Chicago Poems* by Carl Sandburg; copyright 1916 by Holt, Rinehart and Winston, Inc.; copyright 1944 by Carl Sandburg. Harper & Row, Publishers, Inc.: For text and selected Illustrations from "Clouds" from *Mouse Tales*, written and illustrated by Arnold Lobel; copyright © 1972 by Arnold Lobel. For a text excerpt from *Owl at Home*, written and illustrated by Arnold Lobel; copyright © 1975 by Arnold Lobel. Harold Ober Associates: For "City" from *The Langston Hughes Reader*; copyright © 1958 by Langston Hughes. Little, Brown and Company: For an excerpt from "The Duck" from *Verses from 1929 On* by Ogden Nash; copyright © 1936 by the Curtiss Publishing Company; first appeared in the *Saturday Evening Post*, 1936. Eve Merriam: For "Fred's Bed" from *Catch a Little Rhyme* by Eve Merriam; copyright © 1966 by Eve Merriam; reprinted by permission of Eve Merriam, c/o International Creative Management. J. B. Lippincott, Publishers: For "Mrs. Peck-Pigeon" from *Eleanor Farjeon's Poems for Children*; originally published in *Over the Garden Wall* by Eleanor Farjeon; copyright 1933, 1961 by Eleanor Farjeon. G. P. Putnam's Sons: For "Brooms" from *Everything & Anything* by Dorothy Aldis; copyright 1925, 1926, 1927; renewed © 1953, 1954, 1955 by Dorothy Aldis. Paul R. Reynolds, Inc.: For "Hokku: In The Falling Snow" by Richard Wright; copyright © by Richard Wright.

Photographs

Cover: Thase Daniel

James M. Ballard: 30, 46, 104, 288. Woodfin Camp: Jeffrey Foxx, xii, 238; Michal Heron, 74; Adam Woolfitt, 212. Magnum: Burt Glinn, ii, 182; Alex Webb, 14; Burk Uzzle, 60; Eve Arnold, 90, 170; Paul Fusco, 112, 126, 136, 192; Charles Harbutt, 202; Mark Godfrey, 158; Tony Ray Jones, 222; Martin J. Dain, 246; Leonard Freed, 258; Sepp Seitz, 274.

Illustrations

Greg Hergert: 2, 33, 35, 36, 38, 39, 81, 114, 115, 138, 264, 267, 269, 272; Rodica Prato: 4, 5, 8, 9, 49, 51, 53, 94, 95, 176, 186, 191, 215, 228, 230; Mary Sherman: 11, 189; Len Ebert: 18, 19, 55, 92, 130, 131, 132, 134, 135, 146, 148; Wayne Bonnett: 22, 26, 37, 48, 63, 64, 103, 142, 205, 206; Kip Lott: 24, 174, 175, 177, 195, 199, 218, 219; Steve Bates: 43, 100, 160, 167, 248-249, 254, 255; Karen Ackoff: 56, 83, 97, 172, 240, 241, 243, 244, 245; Ken Izzi: 65, 129, 204, 268; Steve Sullivan: 66, 67, 124, 128, 225, 232, 250, 251; Richard Harvey: 71, 118, 139, 141, 179, 217; Leslie Robin: 77, 98, 99, 210, 214, 220; Linda Gist: 78, 79, 101, 106, 108, 109, 150, 196; Carolyn Croll: 163. Ken Izzi, David Sharp, and Roz Jacobson: mechanical artwork.